Med Free
BIPOLAR

Thrive Naturally with
the **Med Free Method**™

Aspen L. Morrow

Foreword by Mary E. Pritchard, PhD, HHC
Afterword by Dr. Daniel Nuzum, ND

Edited by Amy Larson & Hannah Cross

Pottenger Publishing

Boise, Idaho 83616

www.pottengerpress.com

Ordering Information: Orders by U.S. trade bookstores, wholesalers and quantity sales. Special discounts are available on quantity purchases by corporations, associations, and others. For details, contact the publisher by calling (208) 870-9238.

Printed in the United States of America

Publisher's Cataloging-in-Publication data

Morrow, Aspen L.

Med Free Bipolar: Thrive Naturally with the Med Free Method™. 2nd ed. 1st Printing

Print **ISBN** 978-0-9903429-0-8

EBook **ASIN:** B00JMSQ1YK

1. Morrow, Aspen L.—Mental Health. 2. Bipolar Disorder—Complimentary and Alternative Medicine.

3. Mood Disorders—Bipolar Disorder

Cover design by Jenny Fultz, Fultz Design/ Interior Design by Pottenger Press

Author photo by Rob Ayres, Ayres Creative

Aspen Morrow is available for media inquiries and public speaking engagements. To reach her, please go through Pottenger Publishing **www.pottengerpress.com** or email her at **aspenmorrow@icloud.com**

Connect with her on

Facebook:

www.facebook.com/medfreebipolar

Twitter: **@medfreebipolar**

Blog: www.medfreebipolar.wordpress.com

"Here's to the crazy ones, the misfits, the rebels, the troublemakers, the round pegs in the square holes, the ones who see things differently. They're not fond of rules and they have no respect for the status quo. You can quote them, disagree with them, glorify or vilify them; about the one thing you can't do is ignore them, because they change things. They push the human race forward. And while some may see them as the crazy ones, we see genius. Because the people who are crazy enough to think they can change the world, are the ones who do."

Steve Jobs, Founder of Apple

It is time to think differently

DEDICATION

This book is dedicated to my grandmother, MaMére, from whom I have already inherited my fortune: your work ethic, ability to forgive, capacity to dream, and tenacious entrepreneurial spirit. Even in my darkest moments you reminded me to "reach for the stars" and to never give up on my dreams. Thank you!

This book is dedicated to you, the reader. Your need to have it was finally greater than my fear to share. When I was first diagnosed with bipolar 1, instead of my first Hefty® bag of medications and side-effect inserts, I wish I had been given this book.

AUTHOR NOTE

I am an investigative journalist who was motivated to find the answers to my own severe case of mood disorders (bipolar I with schizophrenic tendencies, ADD, anxiety, SPD, and severe insomnia). This book is my culminated research spanning more than ten years of trial and error and self-experimentation. I am not a doctor, counselor, or psychiatrist.

I am just a fully recovered psych patient whom the doctors told would be on medications the rest of her life. I have lived successfully med free for over ten years using the steps recommended in this book for bipolar.

Some of the methods taught in this book have already worked for tens of thousands of people around the world for almost two decades. They are not just my opinion or experience. They have been backed by science and proven by those of us who have been able to fully recover from debilitating brain disorders. They will also work for almost any brain that is not functioning properly, regardless of the diagnosis.

I am strongly for medication in some instances, especially crisis situations. If you are not sure if the Med Free Method™ bipolar edition is right for you, see the quiz on my blog:

www.medfreebipolar.wordpress.com

CONTENTS

FOREWORD
Mary Pritchard, PhD, HHC

I first met Aspen Morrow in the summer of 2013. As a new business owner faced with a successful businesswoman like Aspen, I found myself very intimidated. I thought that if I worked up the courage, I might ask her for some business advice.

And then I found out she had suffered from bipolar disorder. I didn't believe her. I thought she had been misdiagnosed. As a PhD in Psychology, I have worked with bipolar clients. Aspen Morrow was not bipolar. Even on medication, I have never met someone suffering from bipolar who is that put together, that focused, that driven, and that stable. And Aspen wasn't taking any medication!

People don't understand how real stigma still is, and speaking out now after so many years of silence could affect her career, kids' lives at school, and more. She is brave for doing so when she didn't have to. Like any problem she faces in her business, Aspen conquered her bipolar diagnosis with research and zeal. What you have before you is not only a glimpse into her story, but a preview of what is possible.

Skeptical? I know I was. I know bipolar's MO: the ups and

downs, the magical, mystery train of medication -- just trying to find something that works is a challenge. You may find something that works, for a while, but then the diagnosis rears its ugly head again as your body gets used to the meds and they stop working. I have cried with clients who've been told they are faced with a lifetime of Depakote – a prescription drug with side effects that are often as bad as the bipolar disorder it's supposedly treating.

When Aspen asked if I would write the foreword for her book, I warily accepted. As a health psychologist, I am all for a med-free treatment because I believe that many mental health issues are actually the result of nutritional and neurochemical imbalances. For example, mild depression responds better to exercise than to SSRIs. ADHD can virtually disappear once kids are taken off of sugary, processed foods and fed whole foods. Even Alzheimer's disease has been shown to relate to exercise and nutrition.

However, I didn't think I would ever include bipolar disorder in the category of mental health issues that could be helped by nutritional protocols. Too little is known about how bipolar really works in the brain, I thought. It's too complicated a disorder to treat with changes in diet and supplementation, I protested. Everyone knows that a bipolar diagnosis means prescription medication for life, right? But then I read an article that implicated maternal prenatal diet in the onset of schizophrenia, a disorder just as complicated as bipolar. I read another article indicating the importance of nutrition in our formative years (birth – five years old) in preventing emotional and behavioral problems. I thought maybe Aspen was right.

And she is. The more scientific articles I read about bipolar, the more I believe Aspen's approach is right on. Research has shown that bipolar symptoms decrease with improved nutritional protocols. Given that bipolar patients are more likely than those who do not suffer with bipolar to report poor exercise habits, suboptimal eating behaviors and, consequently, lower levels of key vitamins and minerals, evidence that nutritional changes and exercise may help improve symptoms got my attention.

The question was how? How can we use this knowledge to

decrease or eliminate symptoms of bipolar? Yes, we have scientific journal articles that suggest a nutritional approach may be helpful, but most people don't have access to those research articles.

Aspen Morrow has that answer to my question. As a Health Psychologist and Holistic Health Coach, I cannot claim that Aspen's approach with the Med Free Method™ will cure everyone. I know it has worked for a large number of bipolar patients, but there is always the exception to every rule. So when Aspen told me about one of her friends who had adopted just one of the suggestions she offers in this book (just switching out her salt!) and saw a tremendous improvement in her symptomology in less than a month's time, I decided I needed to not only write the foreword, but also recommend this book to my clients who suffer with bipolar disorder.

Is Aspen's approach backed by research? Yes. Is Aspen's approach easier to adopt than a lifetime of medication? I would think so. Will Aspen's approach cure you? It might. Regardless, isn't it worth a try? Don't you owe it to yourself to live med-free and healthy?

Mary E. Pritchard, PhD, HHC: www.EmBodyHeartandMind.

PREFACE
The Only Memoir Chapter I Care to Write

The lights are stage bright in my eyes; I can only see the first couple rows of chairs, but I know the room is packed. A hand reaches out to help me up the three short steps to the podium so that I will not topple on my high and sparkly heels. In my hands is placed a beautifully hand-blown, blue glass tear-shaped award: "Business Woman of the Year" it says, with my name etched across the front.

Each award has a different custom shape, selected by the artist. My breath catches and my knees begin to buckle. A teardrop: the award is shaped as a teardrop! It is *my* shape.

How had the artist known? Did someone tell him something? Paranoia hit in an instant, and the past came thieving back to steal a moment from the present, an attempt to rob me of my future.

∞

I am transported back to art class, seventh grade. Mrs. England is tall, mysterious, and elegant in my young teenage eyes. Enya sings "Sail Away" in the background while we quietly work on our watercolors.

"Every artist should sign their work in a unique way," Mrs. England says. When she speaks, her hands flow like a belly dancer and her melodic voice is as artistic as her work. "I like to add a kind of watermark, hidden somewhere in the painting. Some artists, like Jackson Pollock, were thought to hide their signature within their work. I use a circle, which is personal to me."

I do not have to think. I already know the shape I identify with most: teardrops. My shape is a teardrop from that day on; it becomes a sad symbol of my life for the next fifteen years, and I rain buckets of tears onto my artwork, poetry, and pillows. It is that year that the suicidal thoughts begin, triggered by an assault, and then the cutting, anxiety, and pain that accompanies my manias and depressions throughout my teenage years, only obvious now in retrospect.

I hold the tear-shaped award in hand, shaking, but my mind cannot catch up to the present.

∞

I'm in college now. An image of a different crowd, a different spotlight on me floods into my senses. I stand in front of a circle of degenerates perched semi-circle on a crescent couch. I am in the common room of a crisis prevention center: a holding tank for the broken of every society, a seventy-two-hour "time out" for grown-ups and almost grown-ups. Abused women with black eyes, swollen lips—the dirty, homeless, drunks, drug addicts—society's castaways are pointing and laughing at me.

I am the most pitiful one there.

Brought here by the university counselor who did not know what else to do with me, I am by this time sleep-deprived for weeks: manic, hallucinating, delusional, psychotic, paranoid, and then finally, catatonic. I stand outside the door to the bathroom too afraid to move. Terror, paranoia and racing thoughts reigned.

"They are going to give me AIDS in that dirty bathroom, or rape me, or steal my clothes." I think. "The food is poisoned; they think I can't feel pain and want to experiment on me. There is a bomb inside of me. You quit the track team to be editor of the paper! Loser! Quitter! You used to be able to handle it all!"

Why is everything so noisy and bright? I really need to pee. Art piece finished? What about that paper due for Western Civ? I have to pee. I have to pee. But I can't: AIDS. I will get AIDS.

The bathroom is full of AIDS. I saw something about HIV on the paper – that must be why they made me sign it, to cover their butts if I get AIDS from the bathroom. Where am I again? I gotta get out of here, finals are a week away. Finals. Finals. Finals. Finals." My neurotransmitters a broken record stuck on that word.

My head feels like a broken popcorn popper with an unlimited supply of popcorn. Thoughts swirl, jump, run on top of each other and race incessantly. My brain is a tangled ball of wire: the circuits crossed, intertwined, and electric.

"This place is gross. Rats! There are probably rats in the bathroom with the AIDS. Rats. 'I was crazy once, and they put me in a room full of rats. Rats, rats make me crazy; I was crazy once....'"

My daddy and I would chant that saying and then laugh until our sides hurt. Not so funny now. It is too bad the irony is completely lost on me when it pops into my head in that moment; I would find it funny, like some Shakespearean comic relief: "Rats...rats make me crazy...."

I don't know that I already *am* crazy.

Thoughts race through my head like a train off its tracks, but my feet are bricks, and my hands hang limp at my sides, as useless as empty gloves. Catatonic, too afraid to go into the bathroom, I am rooted in my spot like the aspen tree I am named after.

I pee my pants in front of the faces that smile, which now point at me and laugh. A puddle pools, and I can't even look down. Burley arms gather me up and drag me to the bathroom, strip me naked, shove me in the shower, and poor acid on my head.

∞

I "wake up" in a psych ward over a week later: my missed finals still the first thing on my mind. I don't remember much of that first week in the hospital, but I am told that I was involuntarily committed. I remember a police car delivering me in handcuffs and then being thrown into a room with nothing but a mat and a drain and given a "warm shot in the ass": the heat had spiderwebbed its way into my brain and toes, blotting out the week to come like black ink.

∞

I ask my mom about the woman who had stripped me naked and poured acid on my head in the shower. I thought she had wanted to rape me at first, so I tried to fight her off. Mom says I had gotten shampoo in my eyes when she washed my hair and I freaked out. I was certain it had been acid, and attempted rape, but then again, I was certain the TV had been talking about me in the waiting room and CIA had been scaling in through the windows. I am grateful for the staff and medications that got me out of that psychotic dream, and for my mom, who nursed me slowly back to sanity.

It is confusing to me now that even years later, the sane brain can often remember what the sick brain was thinking, even if it still can't make sense of it.

Two weeks later, I sit in an outpatient psychiatrist's office. It is one of the most defining moments of my life.

"We think you have bipolar," the old dour-looking psychiatrist says, flipping through the chart loudly that had accompanied my file and looking over the medications I am currently on: Zyprexa, Paxil, Ambien, and others. I have no idea what that word "bipolar" means.

"You seem to have quite a severe case in fact, and it is considered incurable. The good news is that medications do help but you will be on them the rest of your life."

"Will I be able to finish my last semester of college, or work?" I ask timidly, shaking and feeling like I have not only just been handed a death sentence but I have no clue what is killing me.

"Yes, but we need to get you stable first. Many people are able to work and lead productive lives, but some with your severity of condition need to get on disability to afford the medications and repeated hospitalizations," he quips nonchalantly, as if he has repeated this prognosis a thousand times. Maybe he has.

It is then, in my already crushed state, that he delivers the worst blow: "You should consider not having children. You can't go off the meds and not risk hospitalization. You can't get pregnant on the meds either, as they cause birth defects, and bipolar is highly hereditary besides," he says in a monotonous tone. "Oh, and you would be in a very high risk category for post-partum psychosis."

Is he really proposing that I should get fixed, as stoically as if I were a dog needing to be spayed? His voice sounds distant and vague and the room closes in.

The list goes on, I remember most but not all: I will be facing more likely hospitalizations, that I am "type one," rapid cycling, sustained mania – words that make no sense to me. I do not understand half of it; but in that moment, my dreams drop like stars to the floor. I do understand that my life will never again be quite the same.

This bipolar thing seems to come out of nowhere. While the world waits with bated breath to see if their computers would handle the change from 1999 to Y2K, the computer in my brain fails the transition. I am only twenty-two years old.

Looking back now it is obvious I should have been diagnosed at eight years old, but I am not diagnosed until my senior year of college. The past looks much clearer in the rear-view mirror.

∞

The next few years play out as if that doctor had looked into a crystal ball. Almost all of his predictions reel out like a bad movie where I am the lead: lost jobs, disability applications, endless med changes, food stamps and public housing mock me in stark contrast to my expensive liberal arts degree, newspaper editing position and internship spent abroad in Japan – all now worthless.

Decades of symptoms: depression, suicidal thoughts, cutting tendencies and more escalate as I get older. My three-month long dangerous manias are followed by months of depression. The juxtaposition between mania and depression is like being able to fly and then having my wings cut off. I feel like a lowly fly who has been turned on its back, buzzing relentlessly in order to turn over and fly again, but pinned by the pressure on my chest and the cloud of depression that makes everything difficult, even breathing.

Any prior hopes of traveling the world as an investigative journalist are dead, and student loan bills, coupled with my past manic spending sprees, threaten to finish me off if the depression and mania don't. My credit is ruined and I cannot keep a job. I am a humiliated college-educated welfare case and mental patient. I, who used to drink and devour books, cannot even read one. It is like my brain has turned to foggy mush. My future looks bleak and I have given up all hope of a different future.

The years of suffering leave me exhausted, hopeless, and broken. I weigh 220 pounds and I am about to lose my husband, my son, my life.

In 2003, however, everything begins to change. I find a natural, effective, simple treatment that allows me to not only get by, but is the foundation on which to thrive! It keeps getting better with time the more pieces I put into place and the more I pursue my healing. This book is the *step by step* how-to book I wish I had been given along that road to med free complete recovery.

The darkness, highs of mania, agitation, rage, paranoia, anxiety, sound sensitivity, and despair has been replaced by light, hope, normal feelings, emotions, and even JOY.

∞

Today, I am thirty-six years old. I am a wife, a mom, a speaker, an entrepreneur, an author, and I have been mostly (one relapse described in book) free of all psychiatric medications for over ten years! I am now free of all prescriptions completely. Most days I am 100 percent symptom-free as well: zero symptoms of bipolar!

I am no longer diagnosable as having bipolar on *any* testing scale. I have been treating myself naturally and effectively for over a decade. The Med Free Method™ evolved over time just for myself, for my healing, and then I enhanced it for my child, who is my mirror. I then further made it as simple and duplicable for as many as will choose to commit to the process.

Most of the methods mentioned in this book I take no credit for: they are other people's stories and triumphs, born out of their pain or genius. They have been primarily discovered by those most motivated to find them: the patients themselves, or the ones who love them. Some of them, like Dr. Campbell-McBride, are doctors themselves who were motivated by their hurting child or family member. After all, it is we who are intimately impacted by the suffering who have the most to lose or gain if the treatments work or not.

What is so hopeful is that **each step in the method stands alone** as effective in the natural treatment for bipolar, but when they are all combined, which is what the Med Free Method™ does, the health results can be staggering! But most importantly, this book is not about me. This book is about you. For many years I thought I was an anomaly, the only one I had ever met who had recovered through natural means. I speak out only now, ten years after finding my cure, because I have now seen thousands healed by the same methods that healed me, and it is time you know about them! These methods work, and the science and the people who recover continue to prove it time and again.

It is time your doctors know about them.
It is time our children and teachers know about them.

∞

Imagine with me for a minute a life without the affects of bipolar. Imagine life without the dark thoughts, dramatic highs and lows, the suicide attempts. Imagine waking up each morning excited to face the day. Imagine a life without doctors, psychiatrists, psychotherapists, blood tests, prescriptions, med management, and the debilitating side effects of weight gain, loss of libido, and the dulling of your senses and emotions. Imagine having no more fear of being hospitalized. Imagine going weeks without even thinking about your illness and how you plan to keep it under control. That is the life I now enjoy and believe you can also!

Think you are too bad off to recover? You are wrong. No one is beyond hope unless they choose to be. What did your life look like before bipolar changed it? What would you like it to look like?

My Before and

After Pictures

2002   2012

Introduction to the

Med Free Method Book Series

DOCTOR'S NOTES — BY ASPENMORROW WWW.TOONDOO.COM

Well, we have done every blood test, tried every medication. Perhaps it is time to try this alternative approach with a 98% success rate?

For every drug that benefits a patient, there is a natural substance that can achieve the same effect.

Carl Curt Pfeiffer, M.D., PhD

Our world is in a health-care crisis. Our soils are depleted of nutrients and minerals, and our foods have less than half the nutritional value of a decade ago. Autism has gone from one in ten thousand just fifteen years ago to one in fifty today![1]

What could it be fifteen years from now?

We spend the most money on healthcare in the world but rank twenty-ninth in life expectancy.[2] Despite all of our science and health-care advances, we are getting sicker instead of better. Despite every new weight-loss secret and guru, we are getting fatter, and so are our children.

Franken foods and chemicals that are outlawed in other countries as being toxic, dangerous, and cancer causing are not only allowed in the US, but the chemicals are being sprayed on our foods and sometimes even injected into them![3]

Most of us take better care of our cars than our bodies; we would never pour sugar into our gas tank, but we readily consume junk food. Our body is a finely tuned miraculous machine that is much more intricate than a car. Then we turn to doctors to fix us when we break down, but they only know what was taught to them by pharmaceutical-funded medical schools. Their every answer is a pill because that is what they are taught. It is not their fault, but that is like cutting off the warning light in a car and saying, "problem fixed."

We know there is a need for change, but where do we go for help? We have to look to ourselves. No one else knows you like you do, and no else cares as much as you. It is time we take back our health. The theme of the future needs to be natural cures and integrative medicine instead of prescription Band-Aids. What is the Med Free Method™? The Med Free Method™ is based on Pfeiffer's Law[4] that states for every drug, a natural alternative exists. But even more importantly than finding a drug substitute, is preventing the need for it in the first place. The Med Free Method™ provides a foundation for the prevention or reversal of hundreds of conditions, and then addresses specific disorders with natural alternatives.

INTRODUCTION

There are over 900 diseases and disorders linked to nutritional and mineral deficiencies, but the scary part is that there is nothing preventing a person from having hundreds of them all at the same time![5]

While not for or against prescriptions, I feel that they mask symptoms that need to be addressed in the body instead of correcting the cause of the disease state. Our bodies let us know that something is wrong, either through pain, discomfort, behaviour, or the way our brain functions; to ignore these cries from our body is criminal. To mask or chemically alter them is even worse.

The Med Free Method™ is a combination of simple dietary changes, highly specialized supplementation, easy to implement ten minute a day exercises, Mental Mindset Recovery, and environmental and detox recommendations to achieve phenomenal results in natural healing and medication free living.

It teaches the reader how to thrive naturally in five steps:

1. Digestive Health: Prepare the soil: water and salt intake

2. Gut Flora and Probiotics

3. Micronutrients for foundational health with additional specific supplementation (like herbs and homeopathy) for lingering symptoms

4. Mood Food & Med Free Diet™, reducing exposure to toxins, and "Accidental" Exercise

5. Mental Mindset Recovery™

The Med Free Method™ can be implemented for almost every body, every brain, and every disease state to achieve extraordinary health benefits.

Here are just a few of the conditions that may be improved or eliminated using the Med Free Method™:

- General Nutrition Deficiencies

- Mental Health Concerns

- Spectrum Disorders

- Autoimmune Disorders

- Heart Disease

In this first book in the Med Free Method™ Book Series, the method has simply been tailored for bipolar disorder, disruptive mood dysregulation disorder (DMDD), and schizophrenia. It can similarly be tailored for depression, anxiety, fibromyalgia, Parkinson's, traumatic brain injury, and even heart disease. By using Pfeiffer's Law and the foundational principles of the Med Free Method™, every brain and body can benefit.

Implementing the steps in the book is not a race. It could take some people just a few weeks, but may take others a year or more, so the book is broken down into four parts, marked by seasons, to symbolize that this is a journey and not to be frustrated if it takes time.

There is a chapter summary at the end of most chapters for those who don't care about all the details, and just want the facts, as well as the action steps. Our primary goal with the Med Free Method™ is to nutrify deficiencies, increase digestive and enzyme functions, increase nutrient and blood flow to the brain so it can function properly, fix sleep, detox, fine-tune through diet and exercising, and then address any lingering symptoms with natural supplement alternatives, complimentary and integrative medicine or further testing. The Med Free Method™ combines hundreds of years of research with the latest and most proven natural treatment methods in an easy to follow, duplicable system, created by someone who has lived it!

HEALING FOR THE *C* STUDENT WHO IS REALLY

'SICK', 'BROKE', 'BUSY' or 'Lazy'

1

Mental Illness is not caused by a Prozac Deficiency

"The doctor of the future will give no medicine but will interest his patients in the care of the human frame, in diet, and in the cause and prevention of disease."

Thomas Edison

I believe that most cases of mental illness are highly preventable, treatable, and reversible using inexpensive natural methods. The medical community, however, portrays the idea that mental illness is a life-long condition that is considered hereditarily genetic and biochemical. As a genetic chemical imbalance it is deemed unpreventable, incurable, irreversible, and permanent.

"The brain chemistry cannot be changed except through drugs. A patient can expect to be on drugs the rest of their life." Experts at the Mayo Clinic state that medications do not address the cause of the mental illness, but simply reduce symptoms.[6] The future of psychiatry is Holistic Psychiatry, already practiced by a few visionaries. Dr. Kelly Brogan, a holistic psychiatrist with a long, impressive resume of helping people recover naturally says,

> With epidemic rates of mental illness in every demographic, more and more individuals are resign-

ing themselves to a lifetime of medication. Unfortunately, this is rarely, if ever, a sustainably effective and low-risk model of treatment. When anxiety and mood disorders are viewed not through the lens of pharmaceutical advertisements, but from a root-cause perspective, insights into the connectedness of different body systems can lead you out of the prescription and endless psychotherapy mill. This information is vital to anyone struggling with anxiety, depression, insomnia, and attention issues and it may very well change the future course of your mental health. Mental health is so much more than a Prozac deficiency.[7]

One in four adults suffers from some sort of mental illness, and one in five children will be diagnosed before the age of eighteen.[8] How did these numbers get so high and what can we do to reverse them? We already know mental illness is rising at an alarming rate, but what does one do about it other than to buy stock in the pharmaceutical companies?

What has happened in just the last fifty years to cause such a spike? Some people say it is genetic pooling, others say it is because doctors are just diagnosing everyone more. While these may come somewhat into play, the real answer, I believe, lies in our eating, farming, and toxic load. These have seen the most drastic shift in the past fifty years and are the only thing that could impact the numbers so greatly.

Our dog foods, cat foods, plant foods, and rat foods have more nutrients in them than our fresh-farm foods and infant formulas! This has led to the thousand-fold increases that we see across the board of health decline and mental health diagnostic cases.

I recently took up a little gardening, and I was amazed to find that in my garden tower, which grows plants from a reservoir of water and vitamin/mineral mixture, by even forgetting one mineral mixture, the plants reacted almost immediately! If the pH was off, or the mineral mixture was too much or too little, then I would get splotchy leaves or a yellow cucumber! We are more complex than a cucumber, obviously.

Just one missing vitamin or mineral in a plant or animal can cause disease, discoloration, or deformity. Humans are no different. We cannot get everything we need simply from a healthy diet anymore, because the minerals are no longer in our soils, crops, water, or processed foods. We have to add more ingredients to the mix. When the body is given the right building blocks, it can rebuild or heal almost anything, as long as there is still blood flowing to it.[9]

I do not believe there is one gene linked to bipolar, but I do believe gene representation can be passed on, or "inherited," which I will explain later. The Med Free Method™ seeks to address and reverse all of these causes, even the way our genes present! Even a "genetic" case of bipolar can be overcome.

You have been told this disorder is incurable. I disagree. The good news for our children and grandchildren is that in many cases, it is preventable as well. It is amazing that mental illness can be prevented in future generations, and this upward diagnostic trend reversed!

Currently, someone with bipolar is usually given three options: "medicate," be "un-medicated," (approximately 75%) or "self-medicate" with things like drugs, alcohol, cutting, self-harm, over/under eating, or engaging in risky behaviors.

The Med Free Method™ for bipolar is designed to simply be a fourth option, one that does not come with the unwanted side effects of the other choices.

What do babies, brains, and parasites have in common?

<u>Both babies and brains act like parasites to their host.</u> As soon as a woman conceives, every nutritional resource in that women's body rushes to attend to the developing embryo. The embryo becomes a parasite, taking the first of the mother's nutrition intake; it does not matter if this were to negatively impact the mother, the baby does not care. It gets fed first.

Just like when it is born, it demands to be fed. After it is born, if it is not fed, it can scream and act out, but while in the womb, it just takes what it needs. If there is not enough for both mother and baby, it will steal nutrition away from the mother's brain, organs, and even strip minerals from her teeth and bones.

The brain operates the exact same way!

In absence of a baby, the brain becomes the primary "parasite". It takes the first of all nutrition, caring little if the rest of the body gets fed at all. Like the baby, the brain does not care if its needs wreak havoc on the rest of the body and it's systems. It demands to be fed.

The brain accounts for just two percent of a human's body weight, but accounts for about twenty percent of its nutritional demands. "The brain when awake demands a greedy share of the body's energy supply: though weighing about 1/50 of the body total, it may use as much as 1/5 of all the energy that is consumed."[10] It takes the first 1/5. The brain, if not getting enough nutrition through digestive absorption, nutritive food, supplementation, or proper blood flow to the brain, it will strip vitamins, minerals, amino acids, and more from bones, teeth, organs, and tissues. When it finally cannot get enough nutrition, it begins to inflame, shut down or act out: functionally (brain fog/forgetfulness), emotionally, verbally, or behaviorally.

In most cases, if the brain is acting out, it means that person is getting less than 25% of his or her daily nutritional needs. This may mean that the diet is abysmal, there is interruption in blood flow, which carries nutrients to the brain, there may be digestive issues interfering with nutrient absorption, or the brain may have been traumatized through a major or minor accident.

"I'm sorry for what I said when my brain was hungry. Hungry brains make for mean mouths." –Autumn Stringam

Most people do not experience brain dysfunctions because their brains are being fed just enough for years. Some people present symptoms early, even in infancy, while others may not show signs until after decades of undernourishment, finally surfacing as mental illness, Alzheimer's, MS, Parkinson's, dementia, or seizures.

This is why every person, displaying brain disorder symptoms yet or not, should care about information on how to feed the brain properly and help it age healthily. Think of many children who act out. They eat sugared cereal with dead milk for breakfast, processed chicken nuggets and fries for school lunch, and discount kid's meal night at McD's for dinner. No wonder their brains are acting out and their behavior reflects their starvation. Their tank is 75 percent empty.

An undernourished brain will act up, and act out. Like a screaming, hungry, demanding baby, the brain must be fed. How it asks to be fed, or what nutrients and raw materials it needs, is the main varying factor. When it is not being fed properly or in high enough amounts, it presents symptoms such as: behavior issues, tantrums, rage, brain fog, irritability, memory loss, concentration issues, seizures, tremors, eating disorders, among others.

For doctor's wanting to label and match something to a drug remedy, these look like the disorders we are accustomed to calling by a diagnostic name: multiple sclerosis, Parkinson's, bipolar, ADD/ADHD, autism, spectrum disorders, seizure disorders, Alzheimer's, and more.

I believe the labels are just various symptoms of a brain acting out, and how it acts out points to which part of the brain is being affected by insufficient blood flow or nutrition. According to Dr. Daniel Amen, who has scanned over 83,000 brains using SPECT imaging, even a seemingly mild bump on the head as a child or adult can cause significant changes to the brain's integrity and affect behavior and personality.[11]

If it relates to the brain, it is usually because the brain is presenting symptoms as a cry for help, for food, or for the raw building blocks that it needs to convert it into neurotransmitters, neurons, and myelin. The nutrients also must be able to cross the blood-brain barrier. Most central nervous system disorders are more closely related than we might think.

When we throw the diagnostic criteria out the window

and just look at the fact that a brain that is acting out or not functioning properly is crying out for something that is missing, it makes a lot of sense. This book could be just as easily titled "Med Free Brain," and apply to everyone with a brain that is acting out, or to anyone who does not ever want their brain to act out by displaying signs of dementia or other disorders. However, we as a society have gotten used to doctor's labels, so thus the book title with a label.

This is why the Med Free Method™ Book Series starts off with the brain disorders. Essentially, they are the toughest to treat. In clearing up mental illness, or now called neurobiological disorder, or NBD, for short, one might suppose that many of the other physical conditions would be cleared up along the way to getting the brain back to health and symptom-free functioning.
A lot of depletion takes a lot of correction.

Before the brain acts out, physical symptoms usually present first, leaving a trail of breadcrumbs easier to see in hindsight. If the brain is not being fed, then the rest of the body systems and organs aren't getting their nutritional needs met either, causing a litany of physical symptoms that coincide or prelude the brain disorder.

Only the most severely depleted individuals experience mental malfunctions. Most people with NBD also have a long list of physical ailments also.

Many of these include:
- Autoimmune disorders
- Digestive disorders like IBS, constipation, or "leaky gut",
- Acid reflux, Periodontal disease
- Poor immunity, reoccurring infections, asthma and allergies
- Heart disease
- Other comorbid NBD diagnoses like: anxiety, sensory processing disorder (SPD), ADD/ADHD, and borderline personality disorder (BPD) – sometimes as many as eight diagnoses at once!

When we start healing the brain, many of the above conditions disappear as well. This was true for me. Long before I had any brain disorder symptoms, I had a long trail of physical ailments that should have served as early warning signs to impending mental doom. Some of these included: colic, throat infections, urinary tract infections, and chronic constipation.

To parents or those not yet diagnosed with an NBD: the physiological symptoms can serve as an early warning light that could point to a future diagnosis of mental illness or other brain disorder like dementia. If you can "fix" the brain, you can often clear up everything physiological as well. Based on the nutritional deficiency theory of mental illness, no one is immune to a diagnosis of NBD, as most of us could be victims of not getting enough nutrients, experiencing a stressful event that sends us over the edge, or contracting a stomach bug that can wipe out nutrient absorption.

"I used to think that people with a mental illness were different somehow. That they had a gene I didn't have, or must have had a traumatic childhood. Then I had a stressful year and ended up involuntarily committed, seemingly overnight! Now I know that no one is immune to a diagnosis of mental illness, even if it runs nowhere in the family. We could all just be one stressful event, one stomach bug, one infection, or one multi-vitamin away from a committal." --S. Parks, Colorado

According to psychiatrist Dr. Bill Short of Community Outreach Counseling, he has seen many women have their first psychotic break and period of psychosis following a urinary tract infection (UTI). Then they go on to recover and may never have another episode. There are very specific reasons for this: basically the infection wipes out the beneficial gut flora and interferes with nutrient absorption and assimilation. The brain does not get fed in the process and acts out in retaliation to being starved.

An animal will act more aggressively when hungry, so is it any wonder that a hungry brain will act out when it is not being fed properly, and quiet down when it gets fed? We see this often in the elderly and homeless populations as well. They are living on the streets or not cooking healthy meals at home, and all of a sudden they are psychotic, delusional, or having memory issues that look like dementia. Give them a few nutrient-dense meals and most of them bounce back quite quickly.

A friend of mine, Victoria "Nurse Savage," consults with seniors and their families and sees this on a regular basis. Nurse Savage says, "I see it all the time in the elderly: they are showing signs of dementia and even mental illness. They have been isolated, eating alone, microwaving meals, and they are just loopy. We get a hold of them for a few days, load them up with vitamins and minerals, and they are fine: brain symptoms gone."

Today, however, as soon as you display even a hint of ADD, sleep deprivation, or depression over the death of a loved one or divorce, you are whisked into a diagnosis and told you need medications. I will show, based on history, science, and new trends in healthcare treatment why the Med Free Method™ should be considered as a viable consideration for the prevention, treatment, and natural healing of Bipolar Affective Disorder types I and II, and the DSM-IV's (the diagnostic manual used by psychiatrists) newest addition to the family: Disruptive Mood Dysregulation Disorder (DMDD). It may also be beneficial for schizophrenia, although we will only touch on that in this book. I will also discuss some new theorized causes of bipolar, who is at risk, and even what we can do to prevent it in future generations! And I will teach you step by step how to implement the MFM for yourself, for a patient, or for a loved one.

The Med Free Method™ for bipolar is for:
- Difficult to treat cases.
- People seeking natural alternatives.
- Those who refuse compliance with medications
- Us who experience every side effect
- People who are treatment resistant.
- Someone whose loved one has a suspected diagnosis.
- A child whom the doctors are hesitant to diagnose.
- Those with comorbid diagnosis (multiple disorders)

- Practitioners wanting treatment alternatives and to be educated for "informed consent" laws.
- Practitioners who want to know what their patients are trying at home.

As well as the base treatment plan that curbs most symptoms, Med Free Bipolar also contains specific natural alternatives for tough-to-treat symptomatic things like:
- Rage, Anger, Depression
- Mania, Hypomania, Paranoia, Anxiety, Nervousness
- Racing thoughts, Extreme sensitivity and Sensory Processing Disorder (SPD) (I call it surround sound or "spidey sense")

There are five steps, and each step is progressive and should be implemented in the order presented to achieve optimal results, although the dietary recommendations can come first, last, or whenever you feel up to implementing the recommendations. Extensive diet recommendations will be covered in the upcoming book: Med Free Bipolar Diet™ and Cookbook.

Surprising results may be achieved with only implementing the first three steps, so do not be discouraged at the thought of making huge dietary changes yet.

"Recovery is a process of reclaiming one's life after the catastrophe of mental illness." --William Anthony

What does it mean to be Med Free Bipolar?

So, what does it actually mean to be a "Med Free Bipolar"? The term is "MED(ication)-free Bipolar," NOT "UN-medicated Bipolar;" there is a HUGE difference. There are a ton of UN-medicated people with bipolar out there who should be getting help but refuse treatment for various reasons; but there are others, like me, who cannot, will not, and choose not to take medications anymore. *Med Free* Bipolar means that you are **free** from the **need** of medications! It means neither you or the people around you

suffer because of your illness. You are *free* from your disorder!
Natural Cures for bipolar as the new century theme:

I firmly believe we are on the verge of a huge healthcare shift. NBD's are the number one healthcare cost to America, and institutions are looking for solutions. According to the Center for Disease Control, "bipolar disorder has been deemed the most expensive behavioral health care diagnosis," with the average psych patient costing over $72,000 per year![12]

Antipsychotics are now the largest grossing class of drugs in the United States, grossing $16 billion in 2010. A friend of mine who was recently diagnosed was given just one prescription that carried a cost of $2,500 per month, and most psych patients are on multiple prescriptions! I have seen one person with as many as thirteen prescriptions at once for her bipolar and schizophrenia.

If this is such an expensive healthcare crisis, why aren't we aware of inexpensive natural alternatives for treatment? How long does it take for a "cure" to be even known to the public, and do organizations really want to find a cure, or just funding to look for a cure? I believe that many natural cures are actually covered up for as long as possible. Read the book Natural Cures They Don't Want You to Know About by Kevin Trudeau for more interesting information on this topic.

A few things that I believe have already been cured are:
- Muscular dystrophy (a selenium deficiency)[13]
- Heart Disease (nitric oxide deficiency)[14]
- Rickets (now known as a vitamin D deficiency)

Scurvy is a good example of a natural cure cover up. It only takes about three months to develop scurvy, and could happen to any one of us without access to vitamin C. Scurvy symptoms include: general weakness, anemia, bleeding gums, loose teeth, depression, skin bruises/hemorrhage; we have all seen the stereotypical images of pirates missing teeth due to scurvy. We could have created a synthetic prescription like vitamin C to profit off of, in fact they did that at first, but eating an orange is easier.

Even when vitamin C was proven superior for the treatment of scurvy, governments and prescription drug developers tried to hide that information! So how long did it take the cure of vitamin C to become "common knowledge" and the medication for scurvy abandoned in favor of a natural cure? This "natural cure" took **264 years** before it was accepted and implemented by the British Board of Trade and put into practice on all merchant ships.[15] Imagine how many sailors died in the meantime.

If the solution to scurvy was so "simple," then why did it take 264 years before it was "common knowledge"?

Just because your doctor is not currently aware of natural remedies for bipolar and mood disorders does not mean they don't exist or can't be staggeringly effective. Perhaps the recommendations in this book will be "common knowledge in a couple hundred years.

> **"When in doubt, try nutrition first."**
> — **Roger J. Williams, PhD (1893-1988) - Hall of Fame in Orthomolecular nutrition**

History of Natural Remedies for Mental Health

Natural remedies for mental illness have been used for centuries. It has actually only been the last few decades that prescriptions have been the only approved and widely used treatment plan.

- 5000 BC—Egyptians were treating mental illness with specific foods, herbs, song, dance, and art therapy.
- 1929—Dr. Reiter from Denmark showed that 23 out of 30 mentally ill patients improved with manganese injections.
- 1930-40—Dr. Francis Marion Pottenger, author of Pottenger's Cats, studied cats that developed behavior and mood disorders mimicking mental illness when fed cooked diets versus live foods, raw milk, and raw meat.
- 1939—Weston A. Price, D.D.S., first published "Nutrition and Physical Degeneration": this book shook the worlds of science and nutrition with its documented evidence of

primitive populations encountering civilization for the first time and adopting modern diets. Research includes some of the first documented cases of mental illness, cancer, and heart disease.

• 1965—Two Japanese researchers, Kimura and Kumura, autopsied brains donated by schizophrenics and found that they were deficient in zinc by 50% compared to normal brain specimens!

• 1974—Linus Pauling said, "The genes for mental illness are likely the genes that regulate brain metabolism of essential nutrients." He highly believed in the use of micronutrients for the treatment and prevention of disorders.

• Carl C. Pfeiffer, M.D., PhD (1908-1988) helped heal over 25,000 schizophrenics in the '70s at his Brain Bio Center, mostly through nutrition and simple supplementation like zinc, B6, and amino acids. 90% could be socially rehabilitated![16]

• In the 1990s, neuroscientists studied the link between nutrition and sleep deprivation in lab-induced psychosis. The military adopted the findings and incorporated them into war tactics. Mental illness was induced and then cured in perfectly normal subjects.[17]

SQUIRREL POINT

Most pharmaceutical meds only need one case study showing slight improvement over a placebo to get FDA approval before the drug goes to market, where the general population is the true guinea pig. In fact, one former pharmaceutical drug rep told me that Paxil CR was the toughest sale she had to make to doctors because it only had a 3% efficacy rating over the placebo! A sugar pill certainly would have been cheaper to the public, as Paxil CR captured about 5% of the US SSRI market in 2002, and grossed approximately $2 Billion in sales.[18]

~~~~~~

• In 1996, scientific researchers and doctors in clinical practice study the effects of EMPowerplus™, a specialized micronutrient blend, on mental disorders such as bipolar disorder. Results have been very encouraging and significant (See Chapter Four).

• Dr. Bonnie Kaplan, a respected behavioral research scientist stated, "If substantiated in controlled trials, the normalization of the mentally ill via nutrient supplementation would be the most significant breakthrough in the field of mental illness since the beginning of time."

• 2004—Dr. Natasha Campbell-McBride first published Gut and Psychology Syndrome. GAPS™ is a landmark publication addressing the root causes and natural treatment for autism, ADD/ADHD, dyslexia, depression, bipolar and schizophrenia.

Scurvy was effectively treated naturally a long time ago. Bipolar can be treated naturally as well. Think of the treatment for bipolar the same way you would vitamin C for scurvy. Apply the remedy and symptoms disappear, remove it and they come back. When you connect the dots between possible underlying physical conditions, salt deficiencies, gut health, probiotics, and micronutrient supplementation, the final results are outstanding health! The Med Free Method™ works for most people, but if it does not work for you, there will always be some latest and greatest drug to go back to and try. Med management, psychiatrists, psychotherapists, and cognitive behavior therapy will always be there to fall back on.

The Med Free Method™ is Needed for Mental Health

The diagnostic standards for NB's continue to expand. Today no one is immune to a diagnosis, as everyone experiences the natural ups and downs of life, or experiences trauma that could be prescribed anti-depressants. The new theme in treatment methods needs to be natural cures instead of prescription drugs. As the big pharmaceutical companies are moving out of mental health research due to the overall lack of efficacy, lower profit margins, escalating liability, cost of research, lawsuits from debilitating side effects, suicides, and homicides, there is a huge need for a new approach to mental healthcare. The situation is getting worse instead of better.

1.   A new approach to treating mental illness is highly needed. Past and present methods for treating bipolar are not creating "zero symptoms." I like the new DBSA campaign that aims to help people with bipolar thrive with zero symptoms. That is the goal of this book as well, but I feel we have already attained that goal! Most doctors cannot stabilize bipolar without the use of medications. They consider it an incurable disorder, and very few people diagnosed with bipolar find true stability on medications. According to DBSA, 25-50% of people with bipolar attempt suicide!

Of the less than twenty-five percent who find a combination of medication that works for them, many discontinue medications due to side effects and/or fear of a shortened life expectancy. Most people with bipolar are not on medication anyway, as much as 75% are un-medicated! Many people never get diagnosed, only fifty percent of people with bipolar agree to take meds at all, and of that 50%, 25% of them give up due to the side effects and ineffectiveness of the drugs.[19] That means only 25% of people diagnosed with bipolar are even "properly" medicated, and MOST of those 25% still suffer from horrendous side effects and breakthrough symptoms of the disorder. New, more effective treatment options are highly needed.

2.   A guessing game and a revolving door of drugs: Doctors try different drugs on patients in what is just an educated guessing game based on symptoms. Most patients have to find a new mix of drugs every few years because a treatment method that worked in the beginning may not work anymore, or dosages must be constantly increased. Many of them, despite the best traditional medicine has to offer, still have episodes that are bad enough to require repeated hospitalizations even on the right medication! Drugs can shorten a person's life span up to 25 years.

3.　　　Children need a med free option. Medications for bipolar, DMDD, schizophrenia, and almost every other psychiatric condition, are NOT meant for developing brains under the age of eighteen, yet they are being prescribed at an alarming rate. Why? Because doctors know of no other option, and many times the behavior in the child cannot be allowed to go untreated. When a child is demonstrating rage and harm to self or others, medication and the potential side effects are preferable to the behavior or potential risk of death. The statistics regarding our children are unacceptable: currently 1,000,000 children have been diagnosed with bipolar affective disorder.

4.　　　There are just too many alternative therapies to sort through. As I found out the hard and expensive way, there are many alternative treatment practitioners and modalities that are somewhat helpful, but for most people not effective enough to result in the drastic recovery I have experienced. Some are downright ineffective, even harmful. Many practitioners are eager to have a difficult case to treat, sometimes even for free, which is tempting to try. Use caution, as some of these modalities could make the psych patient worse instead of better.

5.　　　Side effects from the medications can be worse than the disorder. Risk vs. reward has to be constantly weighed for the psychiatric patient, but often the patient is not even given treatment options or full disclosure on the long-term effects of medications. People are dying due to the disorder, to the side effects of the medication, are in jail or worse due to the homicidal and/or suicidal side effects that are barely mentioned as they zoom past on the TV screen, and then not even mentioned by the doctor. I feel my pharmacist did a better job explaining potential side effects and contraindications than did any of my doctors. One doctor even told me not to read the side effect insert because it might put ideas in my head and elicit a kind of placebo, power of suggestion side effect!

　　　According to the Citizens Commission on Human Rights, long-term use has been proven to create a lifetime of physical and mental damage, and psychotropic drugs can double the risk of suicide. Common side effects of bipolar medications include but are not limited to: homicidal thoughts, depression, mania, psychosis, hallucinations, depersonalization, and suicidal idealization. More serious effects include: heart attack, stroke and sudden death, facial paralysis and tics, and kidney and/or liver failure.

6.   All psychiatric drugs are addictive. Psychiatric drugs can alter the brain and most are addictive: selective serotonin reuptake inhibitors (SSRIs), SNRIs, TCAs, MAOIs, Mood Stabilizers, Anticonvulsants, Antipsychotics, Stimulants, and Antianxiety meds like benzodiazepines. The patients, now dependent and on a revolving door of drug cocktails and given more drugs to help combat the side effects, are left with both the side effects and the disorder's symptoms. Like a lion taken from the wild and then fed in a zoo, the brain's neurotransmitters forget how to hunt and produce on their own, depending instead on the drug that has been fed to them. When the drug is removed, the brain can starve. It is a scary cycle of illness. **The brain has become an addict.**

7.   Medication can hinder personality, creativity, and productivity. Since 75% of people with bipolar either aren't diagnosed properly or refuse to stay on medications anyway, a natural treatment option could allow them to have the best of both worlds: maintain their sense of autonomy and creativity while stabilize the out-of-control behaviors and symptoms. Being unmedicated can be dangerous, as it leaves nothing between you and the disorder. Med free treatment options address the symptoms, correct underlying causes and imbalances, and actually eliminate the rage, mania, and depressive episodes instead of trying to mask them.

The Drug May be the Problem. A litany of cases are coming forward about the psychotropic drugs *causing* the suicidal, homicidal and delusional thoughts. The brain is the final frontier. Do we really understand enough about it to go tinkering with dangerous drugs that alter brain chemistry and cause the same problems that they are supposed to correct? I was never violent, but just three days on one medication and I was homicidal towards my friend over a game of Apples to Apples! I **knew** it was the drug and immediately quit it. Imagine what I could have done with a real trigger like bullying or worse? I shudder to think, and everyone would have blamed it on my bipolar and not the drug!

Kay Redfield Jamison, who has bipolar, is also a professor of psychiatry at John Hopkins School of Medicine and is considered one of the foremost experts on bipolar. She writes:

> My manias, at least in their early and mild forms, were absolutely intoxicating states that gave rise to great personal pleasure, an incomparable flow of thoughts, and a ceaseless energy that allowed the translation of new ideas into papers and projects. Medications not only cut into these fast-flowing, high-flying times, they also brought with them seemingly intolerable side effects. It took me far too long to realize that lost years and relationships cannot be recovered, that damage done to oneself and others cannot always be put right again, and that freedom from the control imposed by medication loses its meaning when the only alternatives are death and insanity.[20]

That statement saddens me profoundly. The fact that most people only have the options of medication, self-medication, or face death and insanity are unacceptable to me in our endlessly abundant world of resources and treatment options. When someone is diagnosed with a mental illness, bipolar in particular, they are given two options: remain un-medicated, and usually unstable like they have been, or comply with doctor's orders for medication management and talk therapy. The doctors get their orders from the American Psychiatry Association guidelines for treatment protocol and the Diagnostic and Statistical Manual of Mental Disorders (DSM-IV) in the administering of diagnoses and prescription meds. That is usually the only tool in their toolbox.

There is a need for change in government funding, grants, schools and institutions, treatment protocols, and in how we think about mental illness and nutritional deficiencies in general. It is the start of a med free movement.

With the Med Free Method™, patients can recover from a supposedly incurable disorder. Jails are less crowded, the streets house less homeless. Lives are changed, and people wake up from their drugged stupor and start changing the world -- artists start painting again, writers, inventors, entrepreneurs, and scientists are able to create and finish projects like never before. They do not suffer from the dangerous highs or suicidal lows, and they do not die from side effects of long-term medication use. Marriages and friendships are healed, and mommies and daddies are reunited with their children.

2

What Causes Bipolar

And How to Pick a Doctor Who Can Fix it

"The disease that has, on several occasions, nearly killed me does kill tens of thousands of people every year: most are young, most die unnecessarily, and many are among the most imaginative and gifted that we as a society have."

Kay Redfield Jamison

Imagine what it would be like to be driving a wagon train, headed out West: dreams, goals, aspirations, and a promising future ahead of you. Then out of no where, a bandit grabs hold of the reigns, takes the wagon for a "joy ride," and then runs the wagon off of a cliff, almost killing you and leaving you to die at the bottom of a dark ravine. Worse yet, your family in the trailing wagons did not see the bandit and thought you ran the wagon off the cliff on purpose!

Bipolar is that bandit.

Some people think of bipolar, formerly known as manic depression, as simply being really happy or sad sometimes. I often hear: "Isn't everybody a little bipolar?" I do not think so, and if you truly had even a little taste of what it is like to have bipolar, you would never say that.

It can come out of nowhere, like a split personality, and make you do things the normal, real you would have never chosen to do. Some people who have bipolar party and drink out of character, buy businesses or cars, rack up credit cards, fly all over the country, get in fights, think they can fly, do whatever you would do if you had no inhibitions, no filters or brakes on your brain. It is at that point not a question of right or wrong, moral or immoral, but whatever your brain wants your brain gets, like a drug addict who never voluntarily took their first hit.

Your brain is designed to have checks and balances, filters and reason. Imagine if those malfunctioned. Imagine actually saying all those things out loud that you think in your head and not being able to help it, watching the words run out of your mouth like Sesame Street® cartoon letters on legs, grasping for them but being too late. It takes away choice, it demands to be fed and paid attention to, and it can destroy everything in its path like a tornado.

It can also be fun and exciting at times, like being able to fly and float, flit on top of the world. Hypomania and mania can feel like the movie "Limitless," where you are bright, creative, witty, and funny. Ideas and creative juices flow in boundless energy, self-motivation is not a problem, but reigning yourself in is. You can wake up rested and excited with only a few hours of sleep, if you can sleep at all. Sometimes your brain just won't shut off, stuck in the "on" position all night, often for days and even weeks.

Sometimes you can hear every sound and see every leaf in exquisite detail. You can feel like you have super powers at times.

But what goes up comes down, fast and hard and terrifyingly so. "Welcome to the 'Depths of Despair'. No one escapes, so don't even try," as it is said so eloquently in the movie Princess Bride. Just as mania can enhance every sensation, depression can rob a person of all reasoning, all light, all color, smell, taste, all hope, and all joy. It can and does kill.

I have not yet formed my opinion about ABC's new medical drama: "Black Box" starring Kelly Reilly as a neuroscientist with bipolar. Vanessa Redgrave plays Kelly's psychiatrist, and although I think it may help shed light on the seriousness of bipolar as a medical condition, I fear it may not do much to alleviate the stigma of mental illness. Kelly will not be able to represent everyone with bipolar, even if she were to do a stellar job representing one person with bipolar.

Bipolar and Snowflakes: No two alike

Bipolar and schizophrenia seem to be two of the most misunderstood disorders out there. It's important to understand that like with snowflakes and personalities, no two people with bipolar are exactly alike.

You cannot stereotype people with bipolar or put them into a mold. This is part of what makes bipolar difficult to diagnose and treat. Thankfully the MFM does not need a specific or even a correct diagnosis in order to be implemented. Throw out the labels and just treat the brain.

Most of us know one or two people with bipolar who readily come to mind, but we know far more who hide their condition than we think we do. Many people wear their diagnosis openly or even flauntingly, like a Purple Heart or badge of courage, while others fear of anyone finding out, like I did for a decade. Some people are doing so well managing their bipolar that you would never know unless they chose to share.

Many people keep their diagnosis (or never get properly diagnosed) hidden for fear of losing their job, health insurance, life insurance, friends, gun rights, facing stigma, and many other very legitimate reasons. They may be your friend or family member, co-worker or even lover, and manage it so well, with or without medication, that no one would ever know. They walk among us undetected, while it is those who are the most extreme in some way that people call to mind first, like the violent ones. This further causes stigmas and stereotypes that only harm. I encourage you to not assume people with the same diagnosis are all alike.

Give each person with bipolar their own fresh slate to be

themselves and do not assume that bipolar will present one way or another just because it presented that way in someone else. For example, my sister and I are from the same lineage: same mom, same dad, similar upbringing, and similar genetics. We are fifteen years apart. We both have the same type of bipolar: bipolar I (pronounced bipolar one), which is often considered the most severe. She and I both had mood changes that are more seasonal in nature. We were both cutters (self-mutilation to release painfully intense emotions), and our suicidal ideations started quite young, hers at age seven, mine at age thirteen.

We have both shared many similar experiences due to our condition such as self-medication with drugs or alcohol, manic tendencies that put us in dangerous situations that led to abuse, and other commonalities. We are both smart and creative: readers, writers, poets, artists, and dreamers.

However, we are also as different as we are alike. I did not relate to her dark moods and constant wish to die growing up. She tended to be more depressed and negative, and I tended to be more hypomanic and manic, but with episodes only becoming really dangerous starting my junior year of college. We are so different it does not even seem like the same disorder when I look at her and she looks at me.

"I wish I could go back to myself ten years ago and give myself advice," my sister said. She still won't take much advice from me, fifteen years out in front, just as I usually do not take advice from my mom. It is a vicious cycle. It is difficult to hand someone a life ring and watch them drown beside you. If you jump in to save them, they may take you down with them.

"Another person's perspective is not necessarily wrong, just different." --Japanese Proverb

Bipolar is characterized by varying degrees of extreme highs and debilitating lows. The highs of mania can last for minutes, hours, days, and occasionally even years, and the lows of depression can follow suit. Rapid cycling quickly goes from one extreme quickly to another, and mixed moods are the worst, where you can feel happy, sad, agitated, angry, euphoric, and hopeful all at the same time, while still wanting it all to end.

It is important to understand that there can be things that trigger episodes, but they can also come on with no provocation, making them difficult to avoid or control. The brain literally has a mind of its own, and judging someone for reaching out for help in any way they can get it is like denying a diabetic insulin. I hold no judgment for those who self-medicate, take whatever medications they can to try and alleviate symptoms, or enjoy their good days and refuse medication altogether.

Feeling sad at situational events like the death of a loved one, a traumatizing event, job loss, divorce, or extreme stress is normal and can usually be healed with time, but people with bi-polar are more susceptible to these triggers and traumatic events could push them over the edge, requiring special supervision or hospitalization.

"My teenage daughter is bipolar and she has ruined my life. I told her she had better be careful, because people with bipo-lar who can't control their sexual urges end up sleeping with homeless people." --Worst thing ever said to me by a friend who obviously did not know my past. Bipolar and its accompanying symptoms and behavior presentations are a medical condition, not a moral or character flaw! This is the most difficult thing for people to understand.

The guilt or pain of things done while manic may not even come until days, weeks, or months later, when coming down from mania feels like falling off a skyscraper and landing on your head into the despair of depression.

Imagine for a second being raped, but then not even "realizing" the rape had occurred until you "woke up" from a three-month-long manic episode. What normal brain does not realize it has been traumatized until three months later? That by itself can be a depressive or suicidal trigger. Oftentimes there are holes in the memories and "black outs" that people describe experiencing. This was true for me.

Imagine a part of your brain looking at another part of your brain and not being able to control it. Imagine feeling like you are having an out-of-body experience, watching yourself do things you would never do, but having no control over it. Unless you have lived it, you can't imagine it.

The depression and shame is sometimes enough to kill, but a depressed state of mind is not your true self either, so it is difficult to imagine an end to the rollercoaster. Up. Down. Up, Up, Up...then Down in an instant or a slow slippery slide. Terrifying, yet somehow fun at times, until you are ready to get off the ride and you find that you can't.

> **"How far do our feelings take their color from the dive underground? I mean, what is the reality of feeling?"**
> **--Virginia Woolf, bipolar suicide victim, 1941**

Most people feel like they can trust their feelings, intuition, or gut -- not so with those affected by bipolar. Often the feelings rule, and are dead wrong.

The most important thing to understand about bipolar is that it is a brain disorder. You or your loved one cannot always control it, help it, or snap out of it. Usually, no amount of talking or positive thinking is going to stop the mania or depression from coming.

Bipolar is a very serious biologically based medical condition and should not be taken lightly. People should not be generalized as being dangerous or immoral.

Those of us who know what it is like to suffer from bipolar or schizophrenia and continue to survive or thrive are some of the most courageous and tenacious I have met. It is a horrible disorder that I feel is one of the most painful conditions of the human race.

For more information on bipolar and a list of the diagnostic criteria, visit my blog:
www.medfreebipolar.wordpress.com

> **"Picking a fight with someone with bipolar is like putting a stick in the spoke of their wheelchair."**
> **–Dr. Phil**

No longer "diagnosable" —

There are those who fit into some if not most of the above diagnostic criteria, but then there is another growing body of numbers, which is where I feel I fit in now: ones who were once diagnosed, but would no longer be diagnosable on a testing scale, or who could get their diagnosis downgraded from a doctor. I am not currently bipolar, I HAD bipolar. I never WAS Bipolar, as that is not who I AM or who I was created to be.

Do I have the propensity for my bipolar to come back? Yes, perhaps. If I do not treat it with the MFM regularly, it will come back, like scurvy re-appearing upon the withdrawal of vitamin C. Like the pirate who was denied vitamin C for a time, my bipolar could come back, just as his scurvy could. Does that mean I am not fully recovered? Does that mean I am not cured? You can be the judge. I really do not want to sign up for that course, take that class, or spend time worrying about the unknown; for today, I am whole, well, happy, symptom and med free. I am blessed. To read more inspiring stories of recovery, go to:
http://www.mindfreedom.org/personal-stories

Would we be better off without meds to begin with?

Most of us have a choice whether we take medications, but that is not always the case with psychiatric medications. Some people are court-ordered to take their medications, and must submit to routine appointments and drug tests. But does the court know what they are doing? Do medications make the situation worse in some cases?
Martin Harrow did a study on schizophrenic patients by following them for twenty years. The twenty-year results showed that schizophrenia patients (and those patients with mood disorders with psychosis) who took antipsychotic medication regularly during the twenty years actually experienced more psychosis, more anxiety, were more cognitively impaired and had fewer periods of sustained recovery than those who quit taking antipsychotic medication. This growing body of fully recovered mentally ill former psych patients has grown into the tens, perhaps even hundreds of

thousands, of patients. Many of them are in "hiding" like I was for ten years.

Most of us who have recovered fully do not talk about it; we live out our lives in the sunshine of normality, haunted by the flitting thought that perhaps our brains could one day turn on us again. Others, like me, are becoming relentless in research and advocacy for change: fighting for those who have not made it out of the darkness into the light of hope and healing.

Begin with the End in Mind: It's Time to Dream Again!

I do not like to look at lists of diagnostic criteria, or go back to those times in my mind where I was sick. I survived only four years of clinically severe episodes, on top of my painful teenage years, and I do not think I would have endured many more. I feel for those who have decades of suffering with bipolar, and I know it is equally hard for those who love them and try and help them.

This book is different. I will not talk about doctors, hospitals, institutions, medication management, psychotherapy, cognitive behavior therapy, or any other main-stream modality, because I went through all of that, and got worse the more I bought into the system.

I had to find the answers on my own, and then lived the results for many years before sharing them with others. You have to picture success before you can attain success, and believe it is possible to recover.

Put to death the option of defeat

But if you deCIDE to do this, then stick to your decision, and tell yourself there is no turning back. Think of other words that end in CIDE like homiCIDE and suiCIDE. Put to death all other options for now, and commit to the process. Do not give up, because it might just be inches before achieving success, like the miner who gave up digging for gold just inches before reaching one of the largest gold veins in history.[21]

"Compared with other mental disorders, the manic-depressive mood change seems rather noble, reminding us of mood changes in the kings of Shakespeare's tragedies."

–Carl C Pfeiffer, PhD, M.D.

What Causes Bipolar Disorder?

Genetic Disorders?

Many people do not believe disorders that are considered genetic in nature can be helped with natural remedies, but there has not yet been a gene linked to bipolar disorder. Since the discovery of genetics, very few diseases have actually been able to be linked to a specific gene, despite all the rumors otherwise. It is the "catch-all" for every disease that doctors do not have a cure for. However, the study of epigenetics has found that even genes can be re-set and "hereditary" diseases altered through nutrition!

What we eat in our pre-conception years (male and female both) can actually affect the health of the next nine generations according to researchers like Francis Pottenger and the book: Pottenger's Prophecy. That also means that what our ancestors ate before we were born helps determine which genes present themselves in us! Their diet and ours affects our gut flora, digestive health, gene representation, immune health, and especially our mental health.

So if a definitive gene has not been linked to Bipolar disorder, then what causes it, and if it is not genetic, how is it "passed" from generation to generation, where we see it run rampant in certain families but not in others? There are many theories, but the good news is that through food, diet, and supplement interventions, even gene expression can be turned off and can potentially overcome even a "genetic" case of bipolar!

Theories of what causes bipolar:
- Genetic Disorder
- Chemical Imbalances
- Thyroid Imbalances
- Blood Sugar Dysregulation

- Hormone Imbalances
- Inflammation
- Adrenal Fatigue
- Inability to Convert Folate (Folic Acid) into Neuro-transmitters (MTHFR gene mutation) (Causing under/over methylation)
- Gut Flora Imbalances /Leaky Gut/Nutrient Absorption/Gluten Intolerances
- Hydrochloric Acid Deficiencies
- Food Allergies/Brain Allergies
- Pathogens like Candida (yeast), Parasites
- Specific Nutrient Deficiencies: usually Vitamin D, Zinc, B6, B12, essential fatty acids
- Toxic Buildup: Mercury, aluminum, fluoride, copper, environmental, food, etc.
- Religious/Demonic/Spiritual/Energetic Imbalances

When asking questions regarding your health, it is most important whom you ask. Each expert and specialist seems to have a different answer. If you ask your doctor, they will most likely say it is genetic or a chemical imbalance.

The next question to ask your doctor is this: how many people in your practice have you helped to fully recover from mental illness? They will probably give you a deer in the headlight look and say that it is an incurable condition that can only be addressed with medication.

That is when you know it is time to find a new doctor. The problem I found is that each time I visited a new doctor, they would take me down their rabbit hole of modalities and elixirs, as I was told to "drink this" or "eat that." I spent thousands of dollars on supplements and treatments. My recommendation is to find a doctor who will support your decision on how to treat your illness, and then pick one method and stick with it for six months, with the help of your doctor. Then, if that still does not eliminate enough of your symptoms, seek out other potential causes or aggravators, such as hormone imbalances, parasites, or food allergies. Some of these advanced topics are covered under specialty recommendations in the back of the book, or in other books under the recommended reading section.

How to find a new doctor that will support your journey to becoming med free:

If you can, find a doctor or nutritionist who will support and compliment your decision to try a natural route to med free mental health, and will give you ideas and resources that augment the ones in this book. Just know that they are harder to find, and they may or may not know about the concepts and resources in this book. They will, however, be able to give some tests to help find the root of your specific situation and help taper you off of medications if that is what you decide to do.

Functional medicine doctors and holistic psychiatrists are the best two categories to look into. Be careful when switching doctors to verify their credentials before using them. Credentialed doctors who are sometimes (but not always) covered by insurance (check your carrier) are as follows:

- American Board of Integrated Holistic Medicine - Locate certified physicians.
- Institute for Functional Medicine - Find a functional medicine practitioner.
- Integrative Medicine for Mental Health - Referral registry and resources.
- Naturopathic Physicians- Check your state for board certification requirements
- Orthomolecular Practitioners- Find a practitioner

If you cannot find a doctor in your area, or would like help with the nutritional recommendations followed in this book, find a qualified nutritionist. They, along with Micronutrient Support (talked about later) can give you the best chance at a full recovery.

- Nutritional Therapy Practitioner- Utilizing Weston A. Price nutrition thought
- Primal Docs - Find a Doc - Paleo-oriented practitioners who incorporate dietary cures into treatment

- Certified Gut and Psychology Sydrome™(GAPS™) Practitioner

You may just go on through the recommendations in the MFM because it is designed on multiple levels to address most issues. Following the recommendations in this book may eliminate the need for many of these tests and correct underlying imbalances. If you are able, and curious, however, these are some tests that may uncover what is going on in your particular case. If your mood disorder has a specific physical root, then the Med Free Method™ can be implemented and then adjusted accordingly. These are some of the tests recommended by Kelly Brogan, M.D. and utilized in her holistic psychiatric clinic in Manhattan, NY such as:

- HsCRP - Tests for inflammatory markers
- Fasting Glucose, Insulin, HbA1c- If blood sugar issues are causing the mood fluxes
- Homecysteine Test/ Methylmalonic Acid - Tests for folic acid and B12 deficiencies
- 25-Hydroxy:Vitamin D deficiency test
- MTHR genetic markers - May indicate trouble converting folic acid and B12 into neurotransmitters.
- Antinuclear Antibody Test (ANA)- Tests for an autoimmune condition
- TSH, freeT3, fee T4, rT3 – Thyroid testing (Not all thyroid conditions show up on testing)
- Hormone testing/ Female Cycle Mapping
- Salivary Cortisol test - To determine proper cortisol (stress hormone) functioning
- Stool Cultures/ PCR testing - Can point to parasites, microbes, and gut flora issues
- Urinary Organic Acid Testing - Helps uncover yeast and bacteria and assesses central nervous system functioning.

Chances are your doctor has performed few or none of these tests. When we look at the body as a whole instead of just a floating head, we see that every system is interconnected. The gut talks to the brain and the brain to the gut, and the heart has about 40,000 neurons and can communicate and even hold memory.[22] If your doctor is not treating you as a whole person, then consider finding another one before continuing this journey into med free health and moving beyond medication for bipolar.

A note on the litany of Complimentary and Alternative/ Integrative Modalities out there:

I aim to stick with evidence-based, science-backed recommendations in this book. However, I open the can of worms on religion and spirituality as it can relate to mental health in a later chapter. In searching for answers to my disorder, I chased after every person who said they thought their remedy might help.

The treatments I have undergone include dozens of modalities, and I discuss a few of them later on, but most of them have been left out completely from the MFM only due to their expense and non-necessity for symptom relief. Most of them hold no real purpose in the foundational healing, but some can augment the Med Free Method™ once near to full recovery has occurred.

For example: I absolutely love essential oils, and use them. However, lavender or vetiver oil never would have brought me out of a truly depressed or psychotic episode, although many people have found relief using essential oils for infections, ADD, asthma, and more.

In your journey to natural treatment, be careful not to spend a fortune trying out every alternative practitioner or supplement claiming to have your cure unless it is soundly backed by proof or clinical trials. Listen to peers who have been through bipolar and recovered or experienced relief, sand save your money for the things that will truly make the most difference in your health.

3

Don't Have a Cow,

Get a Salt Lick

"Our digestive system holds the roots of our health, and if the roots of the tree are not healthy, if they are sickly, the rest of the tree is not going to be healthy. No matter how far or how high away the little branches might be, and the leaves might be, and the crown of the tree might be, it's not going to thrive if the roots deep inside the soil are not healthy."

Dr. Natasha Campbell McBride, creator of GAPS™

Steps one and two are the foundation to the Med Free Method™. Even if you are not a "C- student," sick, broke, busy, or lazy, you still need to read it. But if you are, know that there is a lot you can do on limited time, budget, or cognitive functioning. When I started this med free journey, I went from being an over-achieving college student to not even being able to read. You can only start from where you are. It is best to read the following chapters spread out over several days, or read and then re-read them, stopping to implement each step for at least a few days, weeks, or months before moving on to the next part.

Step One: Prepare the Soil: Digestive Health

When you want to plant a seed, or start a vegetable garden, what is the first thing you should do? Preparing the soil is a good place to start. In this chapter, we will talk about soil quality (our gut and digestive tract), water, air, and nutrient preparation. We have a lot in common with plants, so tend to your body and mind the same way you would tend a garden that has fallen into neglect.

People spend a lot of time talking about eating healthy food, but I have heard of a lot of people who struggle with bipolar despite a very clean diet! They tell me: "If nutrition is the key to mental health, then I do not understand why I am still ill! I eat better than everyone I know!" And if nutrition is so important, then why doesn't everyone who eats horribly develop a diagnosis?

How can it be that someone who eats only organic, or vegetarian, or vegan, or any other supposedly healthy diet can be just as sick, if not sicker, than those who subside on processed foods and sodas? It doesn't seem fair.

> **"A nation that destroys its soil destroys itself."**
> **--Franklin D. Roosevelt**

Honestly, I am sick and tired of hearing "you are what you eat." I knew that already, but my first manic episode came on when I was in the best physical shape of my life. I ate well, worked out for hours a day and still became ill. When I ate better than everyone else I knew: cut out soda, eating out, processed foods, almost everything, I was still sick. I exercised, I drank water, but nothing seemed to help! I eventually gave up running and even preparing meals due to the severity of my illness, and directions on a Hamburger Helper box were difficult to follow. I would read and reread the same sentence over and over, forgetting it as soon as I read it.

Today, people tell me all the time how well they eat, and that nutrition can't be the key, or they would not be sick. I know how they feel. But the investigative journalist in me would not let it go until I had found the answers, and I am still seeking and learning.

Starving after an all-you-can eat buffet

There is a new saying that Americans are highly overfed but

undernourished. We are one of the most overfed nations in the world. Processed foods make up seventy percent of our diet![23] This makes us more malnourished than many people even in third world countries. Our organs, tissues, and skeleton are withering away under layers of marshmallow puff.

This is an easy statement to understand when you look at the Standard American Diet (SAD). I have trouble even shopping at the grocery store anymore when I see what people put in their carts and actually pay money for: food with absolutely no nutritional value whatsoever! I shop at local farmer's markets just so I am not reminded of my mentally ill days of surviving on what could be opened and microwaved easily. Following a recipe was impossible, and I did what I had to do to survive.

But did you know that you could eat a healthy diet and not get nutritional benefits from it? Did you know that some people could eat hardly any healthy food and still glean enough nutrition from it for their body and brain to operate properly? Your body is a fine-tuned machine, and it needs proper tools to even digest food.

I am in no way a car expert, but it seems like the type, grade, and ethanol content of the gasoline you put in your car would have little impact if the car's engine were broken. The purpose of your car's engine is to convert gasoline into motion so that your car can move. Your car's engine is an internal combustion engine, and so is your digestive tract: its job is to break down food and extract nutrients from it so that you can move, think, and function properly. Just like in a car, all the parts need to work together to convert fuel/food into motion/proper functioning.

It makes little sense to put expensive gas into a car with a broken engine, just as it makes little sense to put in expensive supplements or all organic, grass-fed, gluten-free, casein-free, lactose-free, and fair trade certified foods into a broken gut that cannot convert it into proper fuel anyway.

The GUT is your SECOND BRAIN:

> "All disease begins in the gut."
> –Hippocrates, the father of modern medicine

It has only taken us 2,400 years to finally figure this out, but scientists are learning that more than just food digestion is going on in the gut. As much as 80% of people suffering from mental illness also has a digestive issue of some kind like IBS, constipation, or chronic diarrhea. 85-95 percent of serotonin is produced in your gut, and if it is not functioning properly, almost no other functions can work properly either. Serotonin is responsible for many of the functions in the body, but especially digestion.

The Roots of the Tree: Some facts about mineral, nutrient uptake, assimilation, and absorption:

The digestive process is as important to understand in mental illness as the brain itself. If the gut isn't working properly, the nutrition that the brain needs won't ever get there. The enzymes in your mouth are the first step in breaking down food, but hydrochloric acid (HCL) starts the whole digestive process in your gut that helps break down and glean nutrients from food and quality supplements.

According to Campbell-McBride, seventy percent of people with mental health issues are deficient in HCL, and this low acidity starts the whole process off on the wrong foot!

"We could be eating the richest, most balanced, most nutritious diet possible, but if our stomach acid secretion is too low, we may be missing out on much of the nourishment ourselves and instead nourishing the bacteria in our septic tanks or municipal sewage treatment plants!"[24]

Digestive enzymes are also oftentimes low. When food is not broken down properly at step one in the process, other organ functions get overloaded and backed up: the liver is overloaded, then the heart and lungs have to work harder, and eventually the blood-brain barrier can be compromised with toxins.

When this happens, brain symptoms show up in the forms of autism, ADD/ADHD, bipolar, seizures, and schizophrenia. Toxins, microbes, and undigested food that should have been broken down and handled by the stomach and liver can leak through an abnormally permeable gut wall or not get digested properly, leaving nutrients in the food to simply pass through to be eliminated without being absorbed properly or the nutrients utilized.[25]

Putting food or supplements, even nutrient rich food, into an improperly working digestive system is like putting plant starts into rocky, unprepared soil.

When there is sufficient HCL, food can be properly broken down and assimilated for use by the body and brain.

What if many peoples' neurobiological disorders were as simple as an HCL deficiency causing their brains to be undernourished? And what if doctors, scientists, or chemists have already known this for years? The HCL theory explains why Depakote (valporic acid) works effectively, as well as lithium (a salt that also increases HCL production!). This is something that many doctors who prescribe these medications don't seem to understand. And ironically most of all, most psychiatric medications are bound with HCL to aid in the pill's ability to be broken down in the gut and for shelf-life stability. What if it were actually the HCL causing the beneficial effects of the medication and not the medication itself?

Valporic acid (Depakote) is very similar in structure to vinegar and ketones, actually replicating hydrochloric acid in the stomach, possibly making digestion and assimilation of nutrients more effective. Ketones are produced when fatty acids are broken down for energy in the liver, and are utilized in the heart and brain as a vital source of energy during fasting.

Why don't doctors just say, "Depakote is knock-off food for a starving brain, but you could get a similar effect by supplementing with HCL, apple cider vinegar, Himalayan salt, or feeding your starving brain food high in fatty acid like Omega 3s like fish oil or coconut oil that actually induce ketones"? I would be floored if this were to ever happen!

SQUIRREL POINT

Atlantic Ocean vs. Pacific Ocean-caught Wild Fish:

The Fukushima disaster may leave contaminated fish riddling the Pacific Ocean, and since reports thus far have not shown definitive safety or harm,[26] I recommend being careful of the source of fish oil supplements and the fish you eat. Some things to consider in reducing possible exposure to the radioactive fallout:

-Limit Fish and Seafood from the Pacific Ocean

-Increase Fish and Omega intake from the Atlantic Ocean

-Limit imported seaweeds from Japan

~~~~~~

Drugs like Depakote (an acid) may work like hydrochloric acid in the stomach, helping the gut absorb nutrients from food better, but come with a lot of unwanted side effects like weight gain, headache, fever, hair loss, liver failure, birth defects, and more. For me, Depakote literally drained the color out of the world, turning everything sepia or black and white. I also could not feel, not anything at all: no happy thoughts, no sad thoughts, nothing.

I was on Depakote when I got engaged, and even though I thought I knew I had loved my fiancé deeply once, I felt no joy at the occasion, and could not trust my own feelings, a very scary thing. My mind contains the memory of the event, but not the excitement that should have surrounded it. A life with no joy was no life at all. I wish friends and family could understand just how bad some of the medications can be to treat this disorder, and why loved ones often resist taking them. My husband and I recently returned to the spot in Texas where he proposed to create a new memory. It was appropriately emotional this time around, and there was no second-guessing myself. I knew I had made the right choice thirteen years ago and I could trust my feelings. It was a good feeling.

Fortunately, there are ways to achieve similar or even better effects as Depakote, but naturally! Ketones can increase several calming neurotransmitters, and you can do this by taking a spoonful of Bragg's apple cider vinegar before every meal. Sucking on some quality salt (see next section) and drinking a glass of water thirty minutes before eating can also increase HCL production naturally.

Supplementing with HCL can also help absorption of nutrients and minerals, both of which help prepare the PH of your digestive soil to handle the food you eat. Before you invest in neutraceutical grade micronutrients, talked about in chapter four, it is good to get your gut ready to handle them.

Aspen's TIPS: Choose some or more of the following: Salt and water, HCL (taken at beginning of meal), or Digestive Enzymes (taken at end of meal) and Bitter Herbs taken fifteen minutes before eating. These can be useful in improving digestive productivity. Digestive enzymes digest fats, carbohydrates, and any remaining undigested proteins. Bitter Herbs can be a natural way to stimulate HCL and enzymes.

Natural Ways to increase enzymes:
- Pineapple, Papaya
- Cultured/fermented/pickled foods
- Wheat Grass, Yoghurt, Aloe Vera Juice
- Raw, cold-processed honey, Apple Cider vinegar, Lemon/Lime with water

Bitter Herbs:

Bitters "prime the pump" so to speak, preparing your digestive soil for food intake. They increase bile, pepsin, gastrin, enzyme, and HCL production. Bitters should be placed on the tongue; it is still uncertain whether they even need to be swallowed to be beneficial.[27] Herbs, which can be bought and taken in very small doses, include: barberry bark, caraway, dandelion, fennel, gentian root, ginger, globe artichoke, goldenseal root, hops flowers, milk thistle, peppermint, wormwood, and yellow dock.

Take these straight about fifteen minutes before meals. Do not dilute with water. However, they will not work in extreme cases where the stomach lining is severely atrophied. If you suspect your digestive system is severely compromised, talk to your doctor, or read some helpful info on how to heal the gut at www.gaps.me.

"For me, the medications were worse than the disease. Bipolar is hard to live with, but the side effects from the medication were impossible to live with. If my only two choices are medication or no medication, I choose the latter. Forgive me if I will not kill my liver just to make you comfortable around me."
–Brenda Chaplin, diagnosed bipolar I, age 22

Water and Salt: What our cells use to communicate

Imagine a dirty, filthy fish tank: toxic, with the pump and cleaner malfunctioning. The fish don't look so good, but you take each fish out of the water, give it a fish-pill to stop its suffocating symptoms, and then throw it back in the dirty water. Many doctors treat their patients just like this and wonder why new symptoms or issues keep coming up. Doesn't it make sense to first clean the tank, then put in clean water, feed the fish properly so their internal filtering system works optimally, and get the filter working for future maintenance?

What if your system and brain could function well on its own, without chemicals, like a well-running fish tank? Since I do not believe mental illness is a genetic disorder, and that your "chemical imbalance" is nothing more than your brain lacking the right building blocks to be properly fed, let's begin by cleaning the tank. Much of the earth is dependent on salt water, and humans are as well. Water and salt help keep our tanks clean.

How many times have you heard it said: "Drink more water!" I am sure a lot, but you probably have not heard this one: eat more salt! Water and salt make up most of who we are. Our blood is salty, our sweat is salty, and our tears are salty. Our cells and the way they communicate are all dependent on salt, so where do we replenish that salt if not from our diet? You sweat out salt and water every minute of every day, and there are hundreds of different medical conditions that can be alleviated with just salt and water. All salt is not created equal, however, which we will explore later.

The Goldilocks Approach to Water

How much to drink?

We all know the story of goldilocks and the three bears. Think of water intake like that story. You need to find the amount that is "just right" for your body, i.e.: not too much and not too little. Drinking too much water can actually dilute and flush out your vitamins and minerals from food and the supplementation that we will address next, so start today keeping track of how much water you are drinking.

I ran two to three hours per day for collegiate track, shortly before my first episode, and probably just sweated out all of my nutrients, minerals, and salts.

According to Don Colbert in his book, The Seven Pillars of Heath, a person should drink half their body weight in ounces of water every day.[28] For example: if you weigh 200 pounds, drink 100 ounces of water. Too much water might consist of 14 or more glasses of water per day, but most people need to worry more about deficiencies than excess. It is just something to consider. People have differing opinions on what types of water are best, but drinking the right amount is more important than worrying about what kind of water to drink when getting started.

When to drink?

It is a good idea to drink before you are thirsty, or every time you think you are hungry, as usually our first hunger pains are actually a cry for thirst; it is amazing how the "hunger" goes away after a glass of water. When you drink can also play an important role as well. 70% of people with bipolar have digestion issues, and timing when you drink can help that process recover naturally.

You want to get your digestion system warmed up first thing in the morning, and drinking a warm or room temperature glass of water can help get your digestive enzymes going. Adding half of a fresh cut lemon (no short cuts using the plastic yellow lemon juice!) or two tablespoons of Bragg's apple cider vinegar (with the mother on the bottom of the bottle) is preferred.

Drink the other glasses of water in between meals instead of with your meals, as doing this during meals dilutes your stomach acid and enzymes at the time they need to be at their strongest.

Try to drink your daily quota well before bed. Getting to sleep is difficult enough with this condition, but needing to pee in the middle of the night and then trying to fall back asleep can be its own form of torture.

I like to carry a glass water bottle around all day and refill it four times to make sure I get enough water, but not too much. Dropping in a few drops of orange or lime essential oil helps since I have never especially liked plain water.

Don't have a Cow, get a Salt Lick instead

> **"Violent prisoners given unrefined sea salt in their diets showed improved behaviors within a few short weeks."**[29]
> **--Dr. Jaques Langre**

My friends know I could probably write an entire book just about salt. I am fascinated by its history, many incredible uses, and health benefits. I am constantly amazed at how many people think salt is bad for you, including doctors. When most people are admitted to a hospital they are hooked up to a bag of saline solution, which is water and salt. Almost everyone is dehydrated, and our bodies are mostly comprised of water and salt. Our cells cannot even utilize the water we drink without the aid of salt. As I mentioned earlier, our sweat, tears and even urine are salty. All this lost salt needs to be replaced regularly. For an in-depth scientic look at debunking the sodium/salt is bad for you myth, including twenty-five years of medical research studies, read the article: "Add Salt to Your Food Daily – Despite What Your Doctor Says" at articles.mercola.com by Dr. Mercola. Pay special attention to the point that he states that changes in **mood** and appetite are among the first signs of sodium deficiencies.

The good, bad, and ugly when it comes to salt:

1. The Bad: Most kinds of salt are bad for us, even highly toxic, especially the pure white refined stuff that graces supermarket shelves and is placed en-mass in saltshakers in restaurants. Refined salt has been stripped of its minerals (many of it ends up in our children's cereals: "Fortified with 20 vitamins and minerals!"), and contains added aluminum silicate, which is a neurotoxin and has been implicated in Alzheimer's disease.

2. The Ugly: The wolf in sheep's clothing: so-called "sea salt." Not much better than normal table salt, I think it is worse because it is pretending to be a health food. Unless your salt is colored (pink, speckled, black, grey), I recommend not trusting it, as it is difficult to tell if it had been refined: read the label carefully.

3. The Good: "Unrefined Sea Salt" and other terms to look for are: "Macrobiotic," "Hand-harvested, sun-dried sea salt." This salt is not only good for you but also essential that you get adequate intakes of it. Himalayan is the most mineral-rich.

There are many types of Good Salt
- Himalayan Pink Salt (High mineral content)
- Celtic (grey) sea salt, Redmond's Real Salt
- Cyprus flake, Mediterranean sea salt, Alaea, Hawaiian Sea Salt among others. Black salt is infused with carbon for detoxing benefits.

Good salt helps maintain electrolyte balance in the body and also contains a good source of trace minerals. "Salt is the most essential ingredient in the body," according to Dr. Batmanghelidj. Salt prevents acidic build-up in cells and can help prevent cancer formation. Historically, salt has been prized and revered for its healing properties, disinfecting abilities, and high-mineral content when unprocessed. The Bible mentions salt forty times in the King James Version, and cultures all around the world have prized and even worshiped salt.

> "Salt is good, but if the salt loses its saltiness, how can you make it salty again? Have salt in yourselves, and be at peace with one another." –Mark 9:50, NIV

I find it amazing that the Bible, long before mental illness was rampant like it is today, said that if you have salt in yourself you would be at peace with others. Salt can help calm moods, prevent and reverse headaches, and even reduce fighting in marriages, according to John Gray, PhD, author of Men are from Mars, Women are from Venus.

Himalayan Pink Salt

Himalayan pink salt is harvested from ancient sea salt deposits deep in the Himalayan Mountains. It is recognized most for its beautiful color, but we are interested in its high mineral content. It is the one I most recommend. It naturally contains about 84 elements, including macrominerals, trace minerals, hydrogen and oxygen!

SQUIRREL POINT

My Nickname: "Salt Snob", and "Salt Addict": I carry a salt grinder in my purse that my hubby bought me a few years ago. When he bought it, the lady at the counter looked at him inquisitively when he set it on the counter, and said: "Just the one? Don't you want the pepper shaker to go with it?" My hubby said, "No, just the one, my wife doesn't like pepper." The clerk gave my husband the dirtiest look! I guess he must have really messed up their inventory! He jokes I am going to be known as the "crazy salt lady" when I'm old instead of the "crazy cat lady".

~~~~~~

Ironically, lithium is a salt compound, which actually comes in many forms, both healthy and unhealthy, just like table salt. Salt can be toxic, and healthy; lithium can be toxic and healthy as well, depending on the version. Most people with bipolar are highly deficient in salt, so as long as you are eating the right kinds, listed above, have all you want. I even put salt crystals under my tongue to ward off an early headache, and it works like aspirin in most cases.

> **"The cure for anything is salt water:**
> **sweat, tears or the sea."**
> **Isak Dinesen**

The Bipolar Relationship to Salt

Lithium Orotate versus Prescription Lithium Carbonate:

The bipolar link to salt deficiencies has been understood for centuries. Lithium is a salt compound. Lithium carbonate was approved by the FDA for the treatment of mania in 1970, but had long been in use prior to that. It was discovered as an element in 1817, and was used in the treatment of mania as early as 1871.

Naturally occurring lithium-rich mineral baths and springs attracted people for their numerous health benefits, even including the word "Lith" in their establishment name to allure the public. Lithium used to be considered a good thing and sought after for its health benefits. Now it holds a stigma almost as strong as mental illness does.

Natural forms of lithium are less concentrated and are compounded differently than the prescription forms, so side effects are not as great an issue. Trace amounts of lithium are in Himalayan pink salt as well!

I am neither for nor against medications as a strict rule; I am however, very much for you knowing all of your options and alternatives. The doctors can let you know about all of the prescription options available to you, but they may not know about a safe, natural form of lithium.

Although this lithium, called lithium orotate, has not been clinically studied side by side with lithium in actual clinical trials that I am aware of, it has been tested by several of my peers with bipolar who did pretty well for years on lithium carbonate (by prescription), and then transitioned over to lithium orotate (found in health food stores). They found even greater health and stability without the side effects, prescription refills, blood tests, and fear of kidney failure.

If there were a safer, more effective form of lithium that you could get without a prescription, wouldn't you want to know about it? I did, and even got righteously angry the more I learned. The very thought of doctors prescribing the prescription form of lithium makes me sick to my stomach since I discovered a healthy rather than toxic alternative!

NOTE: When using the Med Free Method™, it is important to follow water and salt recommendations. Too much water can dilute stomach acid and digestive enzymes, as well as flush out minerals and nutrients, while too little water will leave you with even bigger problems like constipation and dehydration, especially due to the increased salt intake.

Lithium Orotate (120mg), over the counter

Most people today don't realize that lithium itself is not a drug, but a naturally occurring mineral salt, like potassium. It can be found naturally in Himalayan salt, water, soil, and in fruits and vegetables. Lithium is vital for the proper functioning of every brain.

I often get asked how is lithium orotate different from lithium carbonate and lithium citrate (the ones prescribed)? Lithium orotate is in its natural mineral form, requiring less to affect more results. The body utilizes about 97%, whereas it takes large quantities of the pharmaceutical grade lithium, at near toxic levels, to be effective.

Dr. Hans Nieper of Germany discovered that lithium orotate or lithium aspartate penetrate cells more effectively than lithium carbonate. This means that smaller doses can be used to achieve therapeutic results, versus the higher doses of prescription lithium that borderline toxicity levels. The effective therapeutic window using prescription lithium is dangerously close to the toxicity level, which is why regular blood/toxicity levels need to be checked through doctor supervision.

Lithium orotate is a safe over-the-counter mineral supplement that can be safely used to augment symptoms of:
- Stress

- Bipolar Disorder I & II (formerly manic depression)
- ADHD and ADD, Depression
- Alcoholism, Aggression, Rage
- Post Traumatic Stress Disorder (PTSD), Alzheimer's, and much more

It is said to be effective for 70-80 percent of individuals with bipolar who take it![30] I was scared of this natural remedy for quite a while. Even the name scared me into thinking it was like the prescription lithium, of which I had heard horror stories of kidney failure, blood lithium level checks, and other debilitating side effects similar to what I experienced while taking Depakote.

I encourage you to do your own research, but I have read quite extensively now on this natural salt. I have talked to chiropractors, health-food storeowners, and naturopaths about its safety and efficacy. I can see that it may be amazingly beneficial to many people without the harmful side effects.

For the "broke, busy, lazy, or very sick" lithium orotate could be a first natural treatment protocol if desired, as it is quite inexpensive. It is more effective at much lower doses than prescription lithium because it works on a cellular level instead of in the blood, and is more potent at low doses!

It can also be beneficial for every "normal" brain as well! It protects the brain in a number of important ways, and has recently been found that low doses can actually restore and increase the grey matter in the brain, which is said to be the source of intelligence. It preserves and even renews brain cells. Eight out of ten people given lithium orotate increased their grey matter by three percent in only four weeks![31] Nothing else so far has been shown to do this. Supplementing with small amounts of lithium orotate may also provide anti-aging benefits to the brain, as well as protecting it from toxins.

Lithium can also:
- Block the damaging effects of excitotoxins like Monosodium Glutamate (MSG), aspartame (found in diet sodas), and other chemicals found in processed foods.
- Help form new cells by enhancing DNA replication.

- Help protect against brain cell death caused by anti-convulsant drugs and may protect against damaging effects of illegal drugs, alcohol, tobacco, caffeine, and marijuana.
- May repair the brain's abnormally functioning neural pathways.[32]
- Help chelate aluminum thought to cause Alzheimer's disease (AD) so that it can be expelled from the body according to a 2001 abstract in Society for Neuroscience.

The most interesting thing that I found in my research of lithium was a case study where 27 Texas counties found that the incidences of homicide, rape, robbery, burglary, suicides, and arrests for drug possession were significantly higher in counties whose drinking water contained little or no lithium. Comparatively, places where water naturally contained higher amounts of lithium had lower crime rates, and fewer hospitalizations for mental illness, psychosis, neurosis, personality disorders, schizophrenia, and even eating disorders.[33]

SQUIRREL POINT

James Howenstine, M.D. spent thirty-four years as an internal medicine specialist before becoming convinced that natural products are safer, more effective, and less expensive than pharmaceutical drugs. He is the author of A Physicians Guide to Natural Products that Work, and believes that lithium should be added directly to the water supply instead of fluoride, especially in counties where lithium levels are deficient. Doing so would reduce crime rates, increase longevity of brain function in seniors, and help curtail the staggering number of children who are diagnosed with learning disabilities. "Since placing lithium in our water could improve general health and decrease the need for pharmaceutical drugs, there is little possibility this will occur," Howenstine said.

~~~~~~

Possible side effects of Lithium Orotate: May need to increase water intake. Dry skin may result if water intake is not sufficient.

May become smarter, have clearer thoughts, may provide memory loss prevention, stable moods, reduced stress. May cause irritation or agitation when combined with other mineral-based supplements (see Chapter Four for more details).

Where to buy and how much to take? Lithium orotate can be found over-the-counter at most health food stores and many supermarket chains like Whole Foods, Fred Meyer, and even some Wal-Marts. A typical doctor prescribed dose of prescription lithium carbonate (for bipolar disorder) is typically 600-1200mg daily. This mega dose provides only 113mg to 226mg of elemental lithium. Prescribed types work in the blood so it takes more to produce therapeutic effects.

A 120mg tablet of lithium orotate usually has 4.5-5mg of elemental lithium. A "typical" dose for someone wanting to take lithium orotate for bipolar symptoms would be about two to five tablets per day, or approximately 10-25mg of elemental lithium. But because it works on a cellular level and can cross the blood-brain barrier more readily, it takes less to produce therapeutic levels. As I already mentioned, a major reason doctors do not use it is that blood-level checks for lithium levels using lithium orotate barely register anything, so therefore many think it cannot be producing results. Sometimes we just have to take it and see. After all, it is our kidneys at risk.

I talked to one psychiatrist who said that he has been using lithium orotate for over twelve years for his clients, and typically sees his patients respond with as little as two tablets per day, but some need as much as eight! Three to five seemed to be the average. Taking lithium orotate with folic acid can enhance the brain's ability to utilize the lithium better.

Food Sources of Lithium

Tomatoes, cucumbers, mushrooms, kelp and seaweed usually retain the highest levels of lithium. Apples, asparagus, bananas, cauliflower, cinnamon, lemons, lentils, marjoram, pepper, red cabbage, sugar cane, whole grains, white cabbage and seeds also contain natural lithium. And don't forget the pink salt!!

> "The only difference between you and the crazy person
> locked behind bars is two cents worth of lithium!"
> –Notes from a college lecture

Cell Salts

Cell salts are a homeopathic remedy that can be a good place to start in helping your body heal. They are the homeopathic (diluted and potentiated) preparations of minerals that are the building blocks of our cells and other tissues. They are well absorbed and can have a dramatic affect on mood very quickly. A homeopathic doctor can help you find a combination right for you if you are interested in trying this remedy, or there is a combination of twelve cell salts available called "Bioplasma". Cell salts can help cells balance water, detox, aid in digestion, improve the elasticity of the cells, increase oxygenation, nutrition, and help regulate sodium-potassium balance. Cell salts may help improve everything from indecisiveness to anxiety and mood disorders.

Don't Just Breathe

Speaking of oxygenating cells, "The Breath of Life" is just that: life. We can go weeks without food and not die, days without water, but only minutes without oxygen. It is vital to health however, that we don't just breathe. We often take breathing for granted: in, out, in, out. But paying attention to how you breathe can give clues to your health. Like a fire, the more oxygen you take in the brighter you will burn. Breathe deeply. Shallow breathing uses only the top ¼ to ½ of your lungs and can lead to: premature aging, headaches, constipation, muscle aches, painful teeth, receding gums, agitation, and memory loss.

On the other hand, breathing deeply, filling your lungs all the way, can lead to many health benefits. Extra oxygen is especially important for those with a mental illness because most of us already suffer from digestive issues, and oxygen assists in the ionization process, where food is broken down into nutrients.

Eat mindfully: eat slowly, enjoy the meal, flavors, tastes, and breathe deeply between bites. Breathing deeply helps with vitamin and nutrient absorption! For example, one person who eats a "fast" food meal slowly and breathes deeply may glean more nutrients from that meal than someone who eats a healthy but scarfs it down and breathes shallowly![34]

Breathe for your brain

Your brain requires 300 percent more oxygen than the rest of your body. It is the first to suffer and the last to heal when you deprive it of oxygen with shallow breathing, lack of exercise, and habits like smoking. Phillip Rice, M.D., who specializes in working with delinquent children, says, "55% of delinquent behavior in minors can be attributed to oxygen starvation."

Oxygen is the ultimate food for a starving brain, but something we never think we are depriving ourselves of because we constantly do it subconsciously. Paying more attention to it is essential. Your body is a fine-tuned machine, and oxygen is its primary power source. Oxygen helps detox your blood, which is important in healing, as people with mental disorders are suspected to be overly toxic, so empowering the detox system by limiting toxins taken in is vitally important.

If all this does not motivate you to breathe more deeply, then maybe this will: breathing in more oxygen can increase your metabolism and help you lose weight. It can also help you clear your complexion and give you a healthy glow![35] Breathe slow, deep breaths: in through your nose, out through your mouth, and make sure the air you are breathing is clean. When you feel stress or anxiety coming on, let that be additional reminders to stop for a few minutes and breathe deeply. Read Super Power Breathing by Patricia Bragg for exercises and more information on how important correct breathing is to every system in your body.

SQUIRREL POINT

Running next to a busy road and breathing in car exhaust can undo any benefits of the exercise.[36]

~~~~~~

Point Summary:

Teaching correct breathing can reduce delinquency in children, and simply adding minerals like salt and/or lithium orotate could reduce crowding in prisons, lower crime rates, and increase health. Water and salt can also increase hydrochloric acid production, aiding in the digestion of foods and assimilation of nutrients. Additional supplementation of HCL and/or digestive enzymes may be necessary temporarily to improve digestion. Even the broke, busy, or lazy can improve their health by utilizing free air, free water, and inexpensive high-quality salt and/or lithium orotate from a health food store. This is Step One in the Med Free Method™, bipolar edition.

Step One: Summary Action Plan

1. Every morning: Drink a warm glass of water with ½ of a fresh, newly sliced lemon or ½ tsp. Bragg's apple cider vinegar. Himalayan salt (brine or under tongue) with warm water is also effective. I just suck on a few granules of pink salt.

2. Drink seven more glasses of water between meals and well before bed.

3. Buy some healthy salt, carry it with you if you can when traveling or eating out. It is that important. Replace ALL salt in your home with good salt like Himalayan pink salt. (It is even a great item for food storage!)

4. Get tested if you can (I used a Zyto Biofeedback scanner) to see if you are deficient in hydrochloric acid. If so, use the salt and water and supplement at each meal with HCL with Pepsin, and/or add in digestive enzymes and/or eat bitters before each meal.

5. Breathe. Breathe deeply filling up the bottom of your lungs.

∞ ∞ ∞

Step Two: Gut Flora and Probiotics:

The Roots of Our Health

"Mom said to eat go eat dirt!"

I have actually said this to my kids before, but I will explain why in a bit. Now that the soil of our digestive tract is well on it's way to better functioning, it's time to take it to the next level. We know that our digestive soils are depleted of nutrients, minerals, and healthy organisms like gut flora, but so is the actual soil that our food is grown in. Crops are no longer rotated as much, the land is over-worked, and the nutrients added back into the soil are a fraction of the spectrum that we need to get from our food. Genetically modified, pesticide-grown, insecticide, putrefied, and chemically altered, it's amazing an apple hasn't grown two heads.

An apple fifty years ago contained more than four times the nutrition that an apple today contains.[37] Spinach used to be a super food, yet Popeye's grandchildren today would have to eat 200 cans of spinach to equal one can in his day: in 1948, 100 grams of spinach contained 158 mg of iron, but by 1965, the same amount contained only 27 mg of iron, and in 1973: 2.2 mg! That was just twenty years ago! Is it really any wonder that autism has skyrocketed from 1 in 10,000 to 1 in 50 in these past twenty years?

Are we surprised by the fact that one in five of our children is diagnosed with a brain disorder before the age of seventeen?[38]

Most can agree, including recent studies, that our soil is depleted, but are nutritional deficiencies the only fallout from depleted soils? If the nutrients are not in the dirt to begin with, then they are not in our food.

But what else can happen to depleted soils that we are no longer working ourselves? Many of our great-grandparents used to grow their own food, and were not only eating healthier, but were exposed to microorganisms while working the soil. There are more than just vitamins and minerals in healthy soil, there are healthy compounds and vital organisms: soil-based organisms (SBOs), and Homeostatic® soil organisms (HSOs). Soil bacteria were discovered by German microbiologists during the Second World War, and were used in protecting German troops from dysentery and typhoid.[39]

According to Jordan Rubin, in The Maker's Diet, these friendly microorganisms that used to be prevalent in our soils, on our foods, and in our digestive tract especially, have been mostly eradicated due to our synthetic fertilizers, pesticides, fungicides, and herbicides. We live in an "anti-bacterial," sterile-seeking society, and it is costing us our health.[40]

So what do we do about it? We need to supplement "dirt" and healthy organisms, like probiotics, into our diet. Gardening with organic materials can also be beneficial. Getting back to our roots and asking our great-grandparents how they lived so healthily for so long is also a good start.

> **"Deficient soil leads to deficient bodies."**
> **--Jordan S. Rubin, Author of The Maker's Diet**

We talked a little about gut flora before, but it is important to understand that this microscopic world comprises ninety percent of our physical makeup. Our tissues, organs, and cells make up the remaining ten percent. When gut flora is compromised, the entire system is compromised. It is estimated that 80-90 percent of those suffering with mental illness have compromised gut flora.[41]

Both Dr. Natasha Campbell McBride, who has doctorates in both neurology and nutrition, and holistic child and adult psychiatrist, Dr. Judy T Safrir, say these imbalances can cause most of the disease we as a human race are experiencing today. Gut flora can also be passed down generation to generation, causing the same disorders to present in families! These organisms can even take on personality traits like bipolar! This hypothesis makes sense when we see conditions like bipolar run in families, but we can't yet link a gene to mental illness.

"Our intestines contain trillions of tiny diverse micro organisms, on our skin, eyes, respiratory, excretory organs, and digestive system. The largest colony of these microbes is in the gut. The average adult carries two to four pounds of bacteria in the digestive system, which represents ten times more microbial cells than human cells. In other words, we are 10% human cells and 90% microbial cells, and contain 100 times more microbial genes than human genes. We are sacks that carry around colonies of vast numbers of microflora."[42]

We have a mutually beneficial relationship with these organisms, but there are harmful and opportunistic bacteria as well. Wide-sweeping antibiotics and anti-bacterial hand sanitizer can do equal harm to both the good and bad. We need to help the good flourish and squelch the bad in our quest to clear our minds, heal our gut, and get our bodies functioning properly, physically and mentally.

"When these opportunistic bacteria gain the upper hand, the integrity of the gut wall is breached and contents that should remain inside the gut leak out, causing inflammation in the body and the brain. This results in digestive, auto-immune, neurologic, and psychiatric diseases," Dr. Safir states.

Enemies to your digestive tract that damage flora and digestive tract functioning include poor diet, sugar, processed foods, vaccinations, pollution, toxins, overuse of antibiotics, and drug use (prescription and recreational). Adding back in a wide variety of beneficial flora, especially Soil Based Organisms (SBOs) and Homeostatic® Soil Organisms (HSOs), can make a dramatic difference in your body's ability to heal itself, which is the goal.

Remember that the gut is your second brain? "The brain is not the only place in the body that's full of neurotransmitters. A hundred million neurotransmitters line the length of the gut, approximately the same number that is found in the brain...The brain in the bowel has got to work right or no one will have the luxury to think at all."[43]

When working properly, the gut produces even more serotonin than the brain. It also produces about twenty-four brain proteins called "neuropeptides" that appear in high amounts in a healthy gut.

The gut is also a rich source of naturally occurring opiates and benzodiazepines (yes, the same ones as are included in drugs such as Valium and Xanax). Your body not only has the ability to heal, but to manufacture all the feel-good chemicals, neurotransmitters, and benzos that your body needs, naturally.

SQUIRREL POINT

Sleep is the most important thing to digestive health, so it is no wonder that most people with bipolar also have digestive issues, as sleep is one of the most elusive things for many people with bipolar. I have included an entire chapter on sleep later.

~~~~~~

"Many prescription drugs that affect the brain also affect the gut," says Jordan Rubin. Many drugs, such as Prozac and other brain drugs often divert serotonin from the body to the brain, essentially robbing it from other parts of the body that also require it for proper functioning. The drugs don't produce serotonin, but steal it. This is like robbing Peter to pay Paul, and will catch up to you in other areas eventually, which is why almost all psychotropic medications come with unwanted digestive side effects. Your brain might be better, but at the cost of other bodily functioning. Serotonin is not just needed in the brain, but also helps move food through the digestive tract. With serotonin absent, digestive issues are inevitable.

Both brains, the mind and the gut, can become impacted by the medications taken, causing not only psychological symptoms, but also physical symptoms like weight gain, constipation, diarrhea, and nausea. Anyone on any prescription medication, psychiatric or not, will benefit from adding back in healthy microorganisms. Many doctors are now recommending probiotics taken along with antibiotics. According to Chris Kresser, L.Ac, "Supporting intestinal health and restoring the integrity of the gut barrier will be one of the most important goals of medicine in the 21st century."[44]

The gut not only is the second brain, but houses most of our immune system. If it isn't healthy, then nothing else will be either. Mud pie is better for you than chocolate pie. Go eat dirt, but not from a sandbox:

Probiotics

Now does it make sense why I might tell my kids to eat a dirt-filled mud pie? It may actually be better for them than a sugar-sweetened pie! Soil-based organisms can be found in some probiotics, and are an easier way to replenish likely microorganism shortages than eating dirt. We should have about 100 trillion organisms in a healthy system!

SQUIRREL POINT

As I have been writing this book, my four-year-old daughter actually ate about 32 children's chewable probiotics, with 2.5 billion organism strains per tablet (32 X 2.5 Billion!!), and all it did was give her some diarrhea and a runny nose. The runny nose was most likely caused by a Herxheiemer reaction, or the "die off" effect that can be experienced when detoxing occurs. This can happen to anyone when they start detoxing, making them feel worse instead of better. If you have issues with yeast or other issues and start to feel worse when you start any of the steps of the MFM, it is probably due to this "die off" reaction. Push through it. I recommend slowly adding in and building up to therapeutic doses of probiotics to reduce "die off" reactions, which are caused by toxins dying off; these are the same toxins that may have caused the psychiatric symptoms, so getting better could entail getting slightly worse first as your body detoxes.[45]

~~~~~~

I take about 35 different strains of probiotics per day, in two different products, including a soil-based one (Primal Defense or Prescript Assist) and another one from a company called QBiotics from QSciences (see product resources in back of book). I also try to consume more probiotics from homemade raw milk kefir and yoghurt or other fermented foods daily.

Most cultures around the world have fermented foods, including milk, beans, fruit and vegetables, fish, meats, and cereal grains. Fermenting foods increases the nutritional content of the food, provides beneficial bacteria, and makes the food easier to digest (see the Med Free Bipolar Diet™ and Cookbook for more information, coming winter, 2014).

Step two is simply buying a good quality probiotic and implementing some fermented foods like yoghurt and homemade sauerkraut or naturally made pickled beets.

Step Two: Summary Action Plan:

- Buy a high quality probiotic, or two different brands and alternate them.
  (See products page for recommended brands)
- Eat yoghurt or something fermented every day. Work up to a small portion with every meal when feasible.
- Plant a garden if you want, or just play in the dirt.
- Don't sterilize your home; use organic cleaners with natural enzymes.
- Antibiotics should be a last resort and only in emergencies

Approximate cost for Step Two: Between $5-$90 depending on products.

Is it any wonder doctors have not figured all this out for themselves? I tell people to act like a cow and get a salt lick, go eat dirt, and don't exercise!

PART TWO: SPRING

HEALTH FOR THE B STUDENT WHO IS READY FOR SOMETHING THAT WORKS

4

The Crown of the Tree:
What to Feed the Brain

Feed Me, Feed Me, Seymour!

Audrey II, Little Shop of Horrors

Plant Food, People Food, People as Plant food?

In the famous musical and film, "Little Shop of Horrors," the plant from outer space named Audrey 2 develops a certain taste for blood, and the shop owner, Seymour, must accommodate or risk being eaten by Audrey 2 himself. He finds "rude" people to feed to the plant to ease his guilt of killing, and the plant is happy, for a while.

Our brains are like that plant. It has been designed to be fed a certain way, regularly, and will scream and whine until its needs are fulfilled. Your brain is begging you, "Feed me, feed me!" It will "eat" you and everything around it screaming, kicking, and lashing out until it gets what it wants. It wants to be fed, and not with prescription drugs (although there is no judgment for taking whatever you need to try and overcome this disorder's horror).

Drugs are like giving your brain a muzzle: not an effective way to feed a hungry brain.

No tree, flower, or Audrey 2 can be supported without proper nutrients, and neither can our brains. If you have that image of your brain as the top of a tree, like on the book cover (see if you can spot the brain inside the tree), what you put in your mouth (like fertilizer) and stomach (the soil) is going to directly affect the health of that foliage, and affect its behavior. Sometimes you can be doing all the right things, eating the right food, in high qualities, but the nutrients are just not reaching the outmost branches and neuron pathways of your brain. Audrey 2 was sweet and compliant when she was fed, but, when hungry, became a "mean green mother from outer space." It did not matter how great the potting soil was that Audrey 2 was sitting in, she wanted nutrients and iron from blood, not depleted soils.

Thankfully I am not implying that we should feed our brains blood, but blood is what carries nutrients to your brain, and if that blood is devoid of nutrients, then we need to compensate for that. When the brain's nutritional needs are not being met, the signals communicating between neurons slow down, the membranes that protect brain cells from damage begin to break down, and the results can be decline in both mental acuity and physical functioning.

Step Three: Feed the Crown of the Tree (your brain)

Fatten up the Brain

Healthy fats are one of the most important things to feed your brain. Breast milk is mostly made up of fat because your brain needs a steady supply of cholesterol. I believe cholesterol lowering medications and low fat diet fads are the biggest contributors to brain disorders, memory loss, and Alzheimer's increases. Just a few signs that you are not getting enough of fatty acids in your food include:

- Allergies/eczema (bumpy chicken-like skin)
- Depression

- Hyperactivity
- High blood pressure

It is so important to supplement your diet with essential fatty acids and healthy fats. These include:
- Fish Oil/Krill Oil/Fermented Cod Liver Oil
- Omega 3-6-9's
- Folic Acid
- Coconut Oil and Grass Fed Butter
- Conjugated Linoleic Acids (CLA): These trans-fatty acids have been made into villains, and now the rates of heart disease and mental illness have skyrocketed because of it! CLA's are found in grass fed meat, eggs and dairy products, and they are known to have many antioxidant and anti-cancer properties.

SQUIRREL POINT

The richest source of CLA found so far is kangaroo meat! Should I start an import business? I hear Australia is overrun with them.

~~~~~~

What to stop feeding the brain immediately:
- Red Dye #40 (This can trigger brain fog and a headache in me within minutes!)
- Dairy if you are allergic (Many people with bipolar are dairy sensitive. Look for raw milk if you're a milk drinker like me. I can't drink pasteurized milk, but do fine on raw.)
- Gluten (if you are capable, if not, consider this a hint)

My brain was like Audrey 2, demanding to be fed

In August of 2000, I went off my medication. I was tired of being numbed and blasé. A life without joy, sadness, anger, hope, and even color was not a life I wanted to remain in. When I was on Depakote the world was grey, dark, boring, and monotone.

But off Depakote, just two months later, in the fall of 2000, I had my worst manic episode ever! I was un-medicated and it showed. Replacing the nothingness of medication was the exquisite detail of mania, and I had missed it, oh how I had missed it; I wanted to feel everything! I shook with excitement when a new credit card came in the mail. I flew around the country, partied, was date-raped, started a business and bought a car. One thing was the same as the other; I did not care, I could not think clearly.

It was all the same to me, it did not matter the activity, consequence, or outcome. It was like someone else had stepped into my shoes and had taken my body and brain on a joyride.

My mania lasted a full three months and then plummeted into the worst depressive episode I had experienced to date. I could not get dressed or leave my house. Paranoia and negative voices barraged me day and night saying, "Worthless trash, whore! Die!" My fiancé had to give me money to keep the lights on. He did not know the worst of it and I did not know how to explain.

Then, all of a sudden I was fine again, my usual sane self six months out of the year, like the storm had passed on its own without aid of wind. I got married and we had our first baby. Life was good, for a blink. I started to get sick again that very next fall, like seasonal clockwork. Our house became dark, desperate, and I became angry instead of just the euphoric manias and dark depressions that I had experienced in the past that time of year. I was told the disorder oftentimes gets worse with age and each episode, and that seemed to be true for me until I was able to halt its progress.

I felt like I was lost in a dark storm being knocked around. I had nightmares of being lost at sea. I started to pray, something I had not done in years. In my sleep I was still lost at sea, but I started getting glimpses of a lighthouse. A small, distant, flickering light: a spot to fix my eyes on as the waves filled my lungs with searing salt water and the winds knocked me from all sides. I could sleep knowing I would see a light. The nightmares reoccurred nightly, but then not just at night. I started having visions while I was awake, and each time, the lighthouse was closer. I kept praying. I begged and pleaded for the pain to stop. And then, finally, a reply: I heard a Voice. The Voice was clear and loud and as close in my ear as anything I had ever heard before.

"Hold on. Something is coming," the Voice said.

I knew in that moment there was going to be an answer to the pain. I knew I had to hold onto my marriage; I knew I had to fight to keep my son; I knew I had to find a way out of the anger and depression. I did not know what, or when something was coming, but a flicker, an ember set into my soul. Something was coming, I had been told.

For months this went on, then a year. I had the same dream almost every night: a storm, darkness, and then the light on the horizon. I started collecting lighthouses; no one knew why, and I did not care to share. I put up an ugly lighthouse border all across our living room: I needed the reminder every minute of every day. My husband was busy trying to finish school and work full time. He was trying to survive like I was. Then, in early 2003, I had about given up hope. I was brain damaged from years of manic and depressive episodes, angry, lost, and getting worse instead of better. My anxiety crippled me in public and I could not work. Nobody knew my personal Hell.

I had been downgraded from a college track-star, 3.5 GPA university student and editor of the school paper to a publicly housed, food stamped, and WIC-wielding burden on society. I blushed with shame each time I had to use my food stamp card at the grocery store or wait for hours in the health and welfare department lines. Dirty baby bottles and gross dishes stacked up. I was humiliated, and the way my husband looked at me broke my heart. Where was the ambitious, optimistic, lover of life whom he had fallen in love with? Where was the girl who wanted to travel the globe as a journalist and undo every wrong in the world?

"For I know the plans I have for you, declares the Lord, plans to prosper you and not to harm you, plans to give you a hope and a future."
--Jeremiah 29:11

A phone call from my grandmother MaMére changed the destiny I thought I was bound for. She had read a newspaper article about a girl who had been a college basketball player who suffered from bipolar and was successfully treating it with a micro-nutrient formula out of Canada called True Hope. Her story was a lot like mine. My grandmother called me and asked me if I would consider taking the vitamins if she were to pay for the treatment. I agreed.

I opened the box of vitamins with no expectations, just another thing that would not work, would not help, but would appease my grandmother whom I respected greatly.

The logo on the bottle had a lighthouse on it!

I saw it and a chill went down my spine, followed by a peace and a hope I had not known before. I had not even taken one yet, but I knew that this might be the answer I had been told would come: "Something is coming, hold on." I sunk to my knees and cried when I read the newspaper clipping my grandmother had included in the box. I cried for my past, my lost future, my son whose mother was failing him, for my husband who had lost his best friend, and for the first time in over five years, I cried because I felt like that light might be within reach.

I don't remember all the details of that transition time. I was un-medicated when I started on the micronutrient protocols, which included an older vitamin formula that required taking 32 capsules throughout the day and talking with a support line to track symptoms.

Thankfully I did not have to taper off of medications when I started, as this would have complicated things. I remember the minerals were hard on the stomach back then and I burped them up for hours, but they were still better than any medications I had taken thus far, a short list that had included: Depakote, Zyprexa, Paxil, Ambien, and a few others I forget.

I do remember about a month in, I picked up a book and could read a couple of pages without having to re-read each sentence five times. I smiled at my son and he smiled back, and I started taking more pictures of him.

Three months in, however, is what I remember the most clearly. There was a day when I was at the park with my son and he was giggling as I pushed him higher and higher in the swing. I giggled back, and the future seemed to be full of hope and opportunity for the first time in years. The fog had rolled out of my head, and the storm had passed. It was like I had finally been washed close enough to shore to feel the sand beneath my feet, and I could stand.

I was no longer anxious in public or paranoid people knew of my past everywhere I went. My lighthouse had come and the ground held. My brain had finally been nutrated to the point of acting normal. Brains need to be fed, just like plants and babies.

Step 3: Feed your Brain, not your belly fat

Because it is difficult to completely change dietary habits when your brain does not seem completely balanced, I recommend starting with supplements and then moving on to dietary changes later. When I was extremely ill, I needed something easier to start with than worrying about what I ate, how I prepared my food, or where I shopped for obscure healthy or expensive ingredients. When I was sick, following recipe directions or meal planning or shopping was terribly overwhelming, so it is important to supplement nutrition for the brain, indefinitely for some people.

> **"We are walking Periodic Tables."**
> **–Daniel Nuzum, N.D.**

The Periodic Table of the Elements

Legend: Atomic Number, Element Symbol, Element Name, Average Atomic Mass

1	2											13	14	15	16	17	18
H																	He
Li	Be											B	C	N	O	F	Ne
Na	Mg											Al	Si	P	S	Cl	Ar
K	Ca	Sc	Ti	V	Cr	Mn	Fe	Co	Ni	Cu	Zn	Ga	Ge	As	Se	Br	Kr
Rb	Sr	Y	Zr	Nb	Mo	Tc	Ru	Rh	Pd	Ag	Cd	In	Sn	Sb	Te	I	Xe
Cs	Ba	La	Hf	Ta	W	Re	Os	Ir	Pt	Au	Hg	Tl	Pb	Bi	Po	At	Rn
Fr	Ra	Ac	Rf	Db	Sg	Bh	Hs	Mt	Ds	Rg	Cn						

58	59	60	61	62	63	64	65	66	67	68	69	70	71
Ce	Pr	Nd	Pm	Sm	Eu	Gd	Tb	Dy	Ho	Er	Tm	Yb	Lu
Th	Pa	U	Np	Pu	Am	Cm	Bk	Cf	Es	Fm	Md	No	Lr

Despite our religious, spiritual, or scientific beliefs, all walks of life agree that we are made of the ingredients on the periodic table. We were formed from the dust of the earth. Those ingredients must be replaced on a daily basis. Since we are no longer getting them from our food, mostly due to depleted soils, we need to get them in supplemental form.

Just as soil needs remineralization, so do we. Remineralizing our bodies can even have some of these same beneficial effects like alkalizing our system, chelating toxins, and repelling harmful microorganisms.

> **"99% of the American people are deficient in minerals, and a marked deficiency in any one of the more important minerals actually results in disease."**
> **– Senate Document 264 74th Congress, 1936**

Supplementing with a high quality, neutraceutical-grade micronutrient supplement is the most essential step in the entire Med Free Method™ protocol. For *most, but not all,* I do not believe true med free, symptom free mental health can be widely achieved any other way.

If you have tried a vitamin formulation in the past and it did not work for you, I encourage you to give it another try with the newest micro-formulations, alongside the other protocols in this book. You might not have been getting a high enough dose or were unable to absorb what you were taking due to digestive or stomach acid issues. Or it may be that you needed all the pieces of the MFM working together at once.

There are more independent research studies on micronutrients for mental health than for most of the mainstream prescriptions on the market. Very few doctors are talking about this alternative remedy, but many other books and publications are very familiar with this micronutrient protocol.

"Clearly, the best solution today is to supplement with vitamins and minerals. Recently, the Journal of the Medical Association reversed its long-standing position against vitamin supplements and declared that doctors should now recommend that all patients, even healthy ones, routinely take vitamins and mineral supplements."[46]

So what are Micronutrients?

"Many minerals (e.g. zinc) are important in dozens of Biochemical pathways vital to brain function."[47]
--Bonnie Kaplan

Micronutrients are simply the essential elements of life your body needs to function properly. The micronutrient supplement I have taken for over ten years is a very special recipe of vitamins, minerals, herbs, amino acids, and other nutrients that give your brain what it needs to balance itself and return to normal functioning. It does not mask symptoms; it heals deficiencies. Micronutrients are not drugs that change chemical signaling, counteract symptoms, or dampen symptoms and numb emotions; they are food for a starving brain. Feed the brain and the brain can function properly, but take the food away, and the brain will begin to act up again.

Carl C. Pfeiffer, PhD, M.D., successfully treated over 25,000 people with bipolar and schizophrenia in the 1970s and 80s! He described thousands of patients with bipolar who were able to make a full recovery. "Most of the patients who come to the Brain

Bio Center with a diagnosis of manic-depressive illness and have weekly swings in mood are merely pyroluric. They are easily treated with adequate zinc and B6."[48]

According to Complementary and Alternative Treatments in Mental Healthcare by James H. Lake, M.D, and David Spiegel, M.D., vitamins are essential factors in neurotransmitter synthesis. Minerals are also important for healthy brain functioning, as well as physical performance. People with chronically nutrient deficient systems have enhanced nervousness, fear, anxiety, irritability, depression, and decreased sense of wellbeing. They propose, based on studying clinical trials, that even *slight* deficiencies can cause clinically *significant* problems.

Evidence of Vitamins and Minerals as treatment:

• Benton et al. (1995): Double blind study with 129 young adults who took a multi-vitamin or placebo for one year.

Summary of Results: Statistically significant changes in mood (associated with B2 and B6), improved attention, decreased anxiety, and improved sleep, compared to placebo group.

• Carrol et al. (2000): Double blind randomized study with 80 men (18-42 years) given either a multi-vitamin/mineral supplement or placebo for 28 days. All vitamins were 12 times the daily-recommended intake (DRI).

Summary of Results: Treatment group had lower anxiety levels, as well as perceived stress, reduced fatigue, and increased ability to concentrate. Severe depression scores were significantly improved in both groups.

The Blood Brain Barrier

The blood-brain barrier (BBB) was only discovered about 100 years ago. The blood-brain barrier (BBB) protects the neural tissue and brain from variations in blood composition and toxins. It is a semi-permeable barrier that only allows certain things to pass through it. Elsewhere in the body the extracellular concentrations of hormones, amino acids and potassium undergo frequent fluctuations, especially after meals, exercise or stressful times. These changes in the body can also lead to uncontrolled brain activity.

The cells forming the blood-brain barrier are so complex that they maintain precise control over the substances that enter or leave the brain.

Unfortunately, in people with toxin overload and especially people with an NBD, this barrier can be compromised.[49] If the barrier is compromised, it can lead to toxins flooding the brain that can cause excitability, anger, rage, behavior problems, and seizures. This very thing happened to my middle child. She had seizures five times before the age of three and had to see every field-related specialist in our state, including brain and heart specialists. If I knew the information in this book back then, I think I could have prevented the seizures from ever happening. The steps in this book have been thought through many times, and each one has been selected with care. Skipping even one of the steps in the MFM could change the outcome of your health.

Many substances are beneficial to the body, but if they can't cross the blood brain barrier, then they are not working where we need them to work.

EMPowerplus™ Q96: Made to feed the brain.

I recommend EMPowerplus™ Q96 as a foundational part of the Med Free Method™ for several reasons: it helps fill in the gaps from what you are eating and what you should be eating, but with the important addition of minerals in balanced proportions.

It feeds your brain the substances to help balance brain chemicals naturally using the raw ingredients it needs, and it is formulated in such a superior way that it can be well-absorbed, recognized as food, utilized by the body, and cross the blood-brain barrier. It also has some essential ingredients, like Gingko Biloba and grape seed extract that act as vasodilators in the brain, increasing blood flow, helping deliver the nutrients to the areas in the brain that are receiving inhibited blood flow.

Dr. Daniel Amen helped pioneer the use of SPECT (Single Photon Emission Computed Tomography) brain imagery scans, and has consistently found that inflammation and inhibited blood flow are indicative of people who suffer from NBD, maybe even the root cause.[50] If you are taking supplements that cannot actually penetrate all areas of the brain, improve blood flow, and deliver the right nutrients in the proper and balanced amounts, you are essentially just feeding yourself from the neck down! This is why I recommend Q96 to my "normal" husband, children, friends and family members. I do not want to see them suffer from degenerative brain health and develop dementia down the road, and everything in the formula is good for every brain.

How and why EMPowerplus™ Q96 was formulated

Autumn Stringam's mother suffered from bipolar and committed suicide at the age of forty. Autumn and her brother Joseph were also beginning to suffer from bipolar at the time of her death, and Autumn's father, Anthony Stephan, was desperate for answers that could have saved his wife and would now help his children.

He shared his struggles with a friend from church named David Hardy, who happened to be a micronutrient formulator for the animal feed industry. Nutrition and supplementation for animals are about twenty years ahead of human nutrition, because preventing and curing disease is the only thing that is profitable in the food industry. Animals can move research along exponentially faster as well because they eat what you tell them to and have no placebo effect.

It is unfortunately the exact opposite with human health: there is no money motivation in preventing and curing disease, but there is a lot of money in treating sickness. If animal health worked like our "sick care," a cow's vet bills would look like our hospital bills, and hamburger would be $200 per pound at the grocery store. For almost every human disease or disorder, a similar condition exists in animals.[51] According to Stephan, David Hardy did not know about bipolar, but he knew about "ear and tail biting syndrome" in pigs, which sounded a lot like bipolar. David Hardy had been successful in treating this condition in swine.

"After hearing of the success of this [micronutrient] strategy from David Hardy, an animal nutrition specialist, Anthony Stephan added similar nutrients to the diets of his own children, who were struggling with treatment-resistant bipolar disorder. The results were striking, and the proprietary supplement, EM-Powerplus™, which is recommended for use at high doses, contains 12 vitamins, 12 chelated minerals, and a proprietary blend of amino acids, herbs, and trace minerals."[52]

I have had the honor of meeting and having dinner with Anthony Stephan, where I got to thank him for changing the course of my life and tens of thousands of others.

Autumn and her brother Joseph have both fully recovered and live normal lives now, thanks to their father's miraculous discovery! You can read the entire story in Autumn Stringam's well-written book A Promise of Hope, published by Harper Collins Canada.

According to my own ten years of research comparing and trying other products, Q96 is widely used (boasting 80,000 users around the world), and the most empirically researched and proven micronutrient supplement in the world. It is also completely safe, even for pregnant/nursing women and children, and comes in a berries banana powder for easier absorption or for those who can't, or don't like to, swallow pills. My girls, who are five and eight, take the powder mixed in chocolate milk or smoothies. I was on it through two pregnancies and was able to nurse for the first time while taking it. My first pregnancy was spent un-medicated, and I failed to produce more than an ounce of milk per day for my first born, despite going to great lengths to try and nurse him. My second child I nursed for thirteen months!

There have been over twenty-five independently researched case studies on the efficacy of EMPowerplus™ Q96 over the past sixteen years of use with outstanding results.

Although not intended to diagnose or treat any disease, EM-Powerplus™ Q96 is formulated for the brain, but seems to also work especially well in people suffering with any central nervous system issues:

- Brain Fog, Memory Issues, Brain Injury
- Bipolar I & II, Obsessive Compulsive Disorder (OCD), ADD/ADHD
- Anxiety, Depression
- Fibromyalgia, Migraines, Severe PMS
- Autism Spectrum Disorders

It can be taken to prevent brain/memory issues down the road. In our home it has helped create more peace, less sibling rivalry, and happiness.

Evidence for EMPowerplus™ Q96:

1. Kaplan et al. (2001): Six month open trial with eleven subjects with bipolar types I and II. The mean time from diagnosis was seven years, with an average of having tried ten medications before entering study. Current medications were continued. Seven subjects had a history of hospitalization, and three were severe enough to receive electroconvulsive therapy.

Summary: Symptom reduction was reported as early as two weeks after adding EMPowerplus™. At six months, symptoms were reduced by 55-65%, according to the Ham-D, Brief Psychiatric Rating Scale, and Young Mania Scale. Statistically and clinically significant changes occurred on all three measurement scales. The number of psychiatric medication needed decreased by more than half! A mean of 2.7 medications per person was reduced to 1.0 with EMPowerplus™. In some cases, subjects were able to discontinue all medications, and remained stable 21 months after continuing to take the supplement.

2. Simmons (2003): Observational study of 19 subjects with Bipolar (14 Type I, 5 type II). Subjects took a mean of 2.7 medica-

tions at baseline.

Summary: After EMPowerplus™ was introduced, fifteen of the nineteen improved: twelve with marked improvement, three with moderate, and one with mild improvement. 13 subjects were able to discontinue all medications over a mean time frame of 5.2 weeks (range of three to ten weeks).[53]

There have also been some recent placebo-controlled case studies with EMPowerplus™ Q96 with impressive results.

Placebo-controlled studies are the gold standard in research, and are impressive on "just a multivitamin," as my doctor once said. This should be evidence enough for any skeptical doctor you may have. If not, all of the research can be found online or by emailing me a request.

Although I now only take four to six capsules per day, it is typically recommended that a higher "loading dose" of up to twelve capsules be used in the beginning until nutritional centers are replenished, and then a maintenance dose of about half the original amount, but a minimum of four capsules, even for children because of their growth rates.

Remember that depleted brains cause depleted bodies as well, and brains take the first twenty percent of what you are feeding it. Taking less than four capsules a day could reduce the brain's acting out, but still leave the other organs and systems depleted. Take enough to feed the brain and your body. Taking "just enough" to heal the brain is like filling your tank just 1/5th of the way full and expecting that to carry you all the way to the end of life. More is better than not enough, especially if you suffer from any of the physical issues like tooth bone loss, autoimmune conditions, or heart issues.

If you are able to take more capsules at first you are likely to heal faster. In the beginning, the micronutrients have to get into every depleted nook and cranny to restore optimal functioning, but once that has taken place, the brain can operate on maintenance amounts. It took higher amounts for my brain to normalize and then stabilize, but once it had, I only need "normal" amounts to remain "normal." I now take the same amount as almost everyone else needs, including my "normal" husband and children.

See the recommended products page in the back of the book for how to order EMPowerplus™ Q96 or contact the person who gave you this book.

SQUIRREL POINT

There are a few other products on the market that very closely resemble EMPowerplus™ Q96, but their potency, price, and even higher mega dosing requirements make them more inhibitory, in my opinion. But you should know all of your purchasing options. (i.e.: QuietMinds is still using a much older formulation that requires taking between 500-1000 capsules per month! Hardy Nutritionals and Equilib™ are also more expensive and require more capsules to equal Q96.)

~~~~~~

So what actually is in EMPowerplus™ Q96?

When people look at the nutrition facts, they look like just vitamins and minerals, but all 36 ingredients are vitally important, and their specific amounts are like a special recipe that cannot be off by even 5 percent or the recovery results can change, according to Anthony Stephan. A few of the most important ingredients for brain function are: B12, zinc, B6, copper, choline bitartrate, DL-phenylalanine, inositol, and grape seed extract. Remember that The Brain Bio Center in the 70s was helping heal people of schizophrenia with mostly just zinc and B6. Never underestimate the healing power in a single ingredient.

Vitamins -- All the essential daily vitamins. What some of the most important ones do, according to WebMD:

Vitamin B6 - Functions as a coenzyme in the synthesis of norepinephrine, serotonin, and y-amino butyric acid.
Vitamin C - Essential for dopamine and norepinephrine synthesis. Helps fight inflammation and strengthen immune system.

Folate and B12 - Assist in synthesis and breakdown of mono-amine neurotransmitters. (Four capsules of Q96 contain 4000% Daily Value of vitamin B12, but well within safe upper limits).

Thiamine, riboflavin, and niacin help make glucose, which is the brain's only energy source.

Minerals - All the essential Trace Minerals

SQUIRREL POINT

MYTH: Neon yellow/orange pee = low-quality vitamins. FACT: B2, also known as riboflavin, is what turns your pee bright yellow or orange. The vitamin's name: Flavin comes from the word flavus, meaning yellow. So don't worry if you pee alien colors. Try for daily fluorescent pee instead!

~~~~~~~

Our bodies require trace minerals for proper functioning. Remember that we are made of all the elements from the Periodic Table, and require them daily. Don't underestimate the power of any single ingredient in the formula, but under-stand that there is a fine balance between these elements, and the ratios are precise. Remember the yellow cucumber? It is important to not take other minerals (like another multi-vitamin/mineral supplement) while taking Q96 as it can up-set the balance of the formula. Extra Calcium and Magnesium are fine, according to the manufacturers.

Minerals must be chelated and bound with organic matter in order to be properly absorbed and utilized by the body. The body is not sure how to eat rocks otherwise. Minerals unbound can actually destroy the very vitamins taken with them and even the gut lining.

SQUIRREL POINT

Chelation- Chelate comes from the Greek word: Khele "crab's claw," or to grab hold of, like a crab clinging to something. Minerals can grab hold of toxins in the body and help flush them out. This can also cause some detox reactions where you might feel worse before you feel better.

~~~~~~

In mineral formulation, your body does not recognize rock dust as food, so it must be very fine, and then chelated with a source recognizable to your body, like food or an amino acid. The Q96 minerals are chelated in a 96-hour process and bound with an amino acid. I picture it like a grain of sand in an oyster, where a protective layer has to be bound with the sand to form a pearl.

Most mineral supplements purchased over the counter are not effective enough and cannot cross the blood/brain barrier, rendering them ineffective as brain food, and often have limited benefits in the body as well. Absorbability, amounts, ratios and balance between elements are the most important things in any supplement.

Zinc, copper and magnesium all play important roles in brain functioning.

Zinc - Important for many biological processes including immune system function, metabolizing proteins, and co-factoring enzymes. Zinc levels are usually low in those affected with borderline personality disorder, ADD/ADHD, autism, and schizophrenia.

Copper - Necessary for the enzyme dopamine beta-hydroxylase, which helps form norepinephrine from dopamine. Grey hair is a sign of copper deficiency and should not be ignored.

Precautions: Copper toxicity (way too much) can cause fibromyalgia, depression, chronic fatigue, and more.

Magnesium - Essential for 80% of the body's enzymatic activity, as well as electrolyte functioning. Magnesium is one of the most important minerals in the body and most of us are deficient in it due to our diet. Low levels cause depression, muscle twitching, and restless legs.

Molybdenum - Activates enzymes and aids in digestion and assimilation of nutrients.

Selenium - Important antioxidant. Helps to detoxify the body. Binds to mercury and can "deactivate" its toxic effects in the body.

Food Sources: Yeasts, wheat germ, whole grains i.e.: brown rice Many minerals can reduce rage; calcium calms the system and can help you sleep. All of the essential minerals in the needed and balanced amounts are found in EMPowerplus™ Q96.

Proprietary Blend demystified:

Beyond just vitamins and minerals, each ingredient in the proprietary blend has a purpose in the body and brain.

Choline bitartrate - Choline is a part of the vitamin B-complex family. It plays an important part in proper brain functioning and the nervous system, helps form cell membranes, aids muscle movement, and plays a role in coordination. May help Dyspraxia (see Squirrel Point below). It may even prevent arteriosclerosis and memory problems like dementia and Alzheimer's. It may also reduce the risk of breast and colon cancer. Athletes use it to improve performance and coordination.

Insufficient amounts in pregnant women can cause: premature births, memory development problems in the fetus, and other congenital defects.

Possible Use in Q96: Can reduce racing thoughts, improve memory and coordination.

Food Sources: Egg yolks (especially raw), meat, and peanuts

SQUIRREL POINT

Dyspraxia is diagnosable clumsiness! Many people with mental disorders suffer from lack of coordination, are unusually accident-prone, and sometimes "trip over their own feet." This is quite common across bipolar, ADD/ADHD, autism, Asperger's, and dyslexia. This is not their fault, but can be attributed to low levels of choline bitartrate (found in Q96) and other nutrients that play a role in coordination and peripheral vision. Both my daughter and I suffer from this condition, but supplementing with choline in Q96 and eating more eggs has helped avoid bruises, accidents, and fender benders.

~~~~~~

DL-phenylalanine - An amino acid, protein's building blocks. According to WebMD, the body uses phenylalanine to make chemical messengers, but it is not yet known exactly how it works.

Uses: depression, ADHD, Parkinson's disease (do not take with Parkinson medication Levodopa), chronic pain, vitiligo (a skin disease), osteoarthritis, rheumatoid arthritis, and alcohol withdrawal symptoms.

Food Sources: Meat, fish, eggs, cheese, and milk (especially raw).

Citrus bioflavonoids - An anti-oxidant that increases effectiveness of vitamin C. Acts as a free radical scavenger. Free radicals can damage brain and other cells.

Food Sources: Raw red bell peppers, strawberries, citrus fruits, broccoli, Brussels sprouts, tropical fruits, garlic, spinach, and green tea.

Inositol - The best way to describe inositol is that it is a vitamin-B-like substance. It works to help balance certain chemicals in the body, enhances nutrient transfer across cell membranes, and aids in conversion of fats. Inositol is essential for healthy cell membranes and to support messenger chemicals throughout the body. Could Inositol be a "secret ingredient" way to balance out "imbalanced brain chemistry"? There are high concentrations of this compound in the stomach, kidney, spleen, liver, brain, and heart.

Uses: high cholesterol, diabetic nerve pain, panic disorder, insomnia, cancer, depression, schizophrenia, Alzheimer's, ADHD, autism, hair growth, psoriasis (skin condition), and can even treat side effects of lithium medication in bipolar.

My experience: Inositol seems to make people "nice" quickly. I have seen a friend sit down on my couch weeping, anxious, and three minutes after I hand them one teaspoon of inositol powder mixed in water, they are like, "Wow, I feel better!" For me, I occasionally get break-through symptoms of anxiety and noise hypersensitivity (SPD), and inositol is miraculous in calming my nerves almost instantly. The "surround sound" goes away and it no longer feels like the sounds are stabbing me in the cells. This one single ingredient has such profound effects for me that it is no wonder when combined with 35 other ingredients, each having their own purpose and goal in the brain and body, that Q96 can be as effective, if not more so, than most prescription drugs!

Food Sources: beef heart, desiccated liver, lecithin oil, lecithin granules, liver, brown rice, wheat germ, cereals, citrus fruits, nuts, molasses, green leafy vegetables, and whole grain bread. Inositol is also found in cereals and vegetables in a form known as phytic acid, which is a combination of inositol and phosphorus. Phytic acid however, should be neutralized in grains by soaking and adding yoghurt to grains or flour, as phytic acid may inhibit certain minerals in the body from effectively working.[54]

L-glutamine - The most abundant amino acid found naturally in the body. It is produced in the muscles and distributed by the blood to the organs that need it. It appears to aid gut function, the immune system, and other processes, especially under stress. Glutamine is needed to make other chemicals in the body such as amino acids and glucose: the brain's primary food. It also helps your body produce glutathione, a key antioxidant nutrient, ensures proper acid-base balance in your body, and maintains the health of your intestinal tract

Uses: To counteract side effects of medical treatments such as diarrhea from cancer treatments and more. It is used to protect the immune system and digestive system, can improve recovery after surgeries, and can increase well being in people who have suffered a trauma. It can also aid in infection prevention in people with a critical illness. It is additionally beneficial for depression, moodiness, irritability, anxiety, ADHD, and insomnia, according to WebMD.

Food Sources: Most high-protein foods including beef, chicken, fish, beans, and dairy products.

L-methionine - Another essential amino acid, L-methionine is essential for heart and nervous system function. It can also possibly help detox medications and clean the liver and blood.

Uses: Liver detoxification. L-Methionine can also detoxify metal content in the blood. Aids in production of creatine, a nutrient needed for the muscles and the cardiovascular system to function well.

Food Sources: raw egg whites and cheese are the highest sources, followed by fish and shellfish, then other meats, raw and dried spirulina and other seaweeds, then turnip greens, spinach, asparagus, bamboo shoots, raw zucchini, and raw watercress, as well as some in sesame seed flour.

Plants as People Food

Grape seed extract (GSE) - GSE helps protect the brain, according to researchers. It aids in strengthening capillary walls, and increases blood flow to all areas of the body. But perhaps most importantly, GSE is one of the few antioxidants capable of crossing the blood-brain barrier, which is a selectively permeable membrane that prevents harmful toxins from reaching the brain. This allows the benefits to be utilized by the brain and central nervous system. It is also an antioxidant that may help lower cholesterol and improve circulation. According to a recent study published by University of Colorado Cancer Center, GSE can effectively target cancer cells without damaging healthy cells. GSE may be an effective preventative cancer treatment, but it is even more effective in reversing late-stage colorectal (colon or bowel) cancer.

Precautions: It can interact with blood thinners.

Gingko Biloba leaf extract - One of the oldest living tree species, it was first documented medicinally over 5,000 years ago to prevent memory loss, and to date has had over 400 scientific studies conducted on it. According to the Mayo Clinic, it may help with leg cramping (claudication), Alzheimer's, memory problems, PMS, concentration, headaches, anxiety, and depression. Although unknown exactly how it works, it may decrease mania in bipolar. According to Jim Haggerty, M.D., in an article in PsychCentral, gingko increases blood flow to the brain, and by doing so, the brain receives a higher concentration of oxygen and nutrients, which has been found to reduce manic symptoms. It may also improve choline (a neurotransmitter) uptake in the brain and provide anti-oxidant effects to neurons in the brain, as well as greater synaptic signaling in the brain. According to AlphaGenetics, this "would seemingly benefit those suffering from brain disorders such as bipolar disorder".[55]

Precautions: It can interact with blood thinners.

Germanium sesquioxide (GS) (organic form) - Do not confuse this with the inorganic forms that are cautioned against. GS is a trace element discovered in 1886 and can be found in nature as well as our food supply, but in very small amounts. GS is being hailed as a nutritional treatment of cancer, but can be toxic against many forms of bacteria as well. It works by boosting the body's immune system and improving the body's oxygen supply. It can help deliver oxygen into the cells. It has been used to treat depression, arthritis and heavy metal toxicity. For the most complete information go to:

www.germaniumsesquioxide.com.

Food Sources: Garlic, ginseng, comfrey, and aloe -- although amounts vary depending on the soil quality. Adding germanium to the soil increases uptake and plant growth.

Boron - Another trace mineral, boron, aids estrogen production, but is especially important in many brain functions, including visual perception, short-term memory, eye to hand coordination, logic, fine motor skills, and concentration. It can also protect the body from parasitic attacks, including, but not limited to, Candida Albicans and help fight off other fungal infections.

Food Sources: Apples, oranges, grapes, kiwi, pears, vegetables, nuts, and dates

Vanadium - Trace mineral that helps lift "brain fog," common complaint amongst sufferers of mental illness and the overstressed public in general. Helps balance blood sugar, and may help reduce the production of bad cholesterol.

Food Sources: Whole grains, carrots, cabbage, mushrooms, parsley, and other vegetables.

Nickel - Needed only in small amounts, nickel is found in your DNA and RNA, which make up every cell in your body, according to Acucell.com, a cellular nutrition informational website. It contributes to the breakdown of glucose for energy, which is primarily used by the brain as food.

Food Sources: Chocolate, soybeans, nuts and oatmeal

SQUIRREL POINT

Remember that many of our food sources are now devoid of proper nutrients and essential minerals, so getting all of your essential vitamins and minerals from food sources may be hard to measure. Whole food supplements seem like a good thing and are currently all the rage, but as mentioned before, an apple just isn't what it used to be. I have used myself as a guinea pig, trying all the latest and greatest supplements to come on the market and I usually get break through bipolar symptoms even after just three days of experimentation, even on supposedly superior plant based or whole food based supplements. For me, the proof is in my sanity. Most people do not have a straight jacket waiting for them if their product does not work. That is quite a measuring stick to tell if a product works in the brain or not!

~~~~~~

Before implementing the micronutrient formula into your diet, it is important to understand that EMPowerplus™ Q96 can interact with medications that you may be taking, so please read Chapter Five before talking to your doctor or loved ones about implementing Step 3 in the Med Free Meth-od if you are currently on prescriptions. Because it looks like just vitamins and minerals but is potent in the brain, it is un-assumingly so affective in balancing out brain chemistry that as it "normalizes" the brain, the medications can quickly be-come problematic. Just as a normal brain should not be on psych meds, a "normalizing" brain on Q96 can become overmedicated due to the psych meds.

Thankfully you can heal without a definitive cause or diagnosis, because when you feed your body what it needs, it will sort out where it needs to go and what to heal. It is not that way with prescription drugs; they need to first get the diagnosis right to assign the appropriate drug, it is often hit or miss, trial and error, speculation in psychiatry without clear scientific processes.

We do not need to diagnose or treat conditions with the Med Free Method™; when you feed your mind and body what it is made of: water, salt, oxygen, vitamins and minerals, and fats, your body takes care of the rest.

Review of steps one through three:

Supplements: (See Product Resources back of book)

1. Take daily on an empty stomach AM or PM: A high-quality probiotic like QBiotics and/or a soil-based probiotic.

2. Take twice daily with breakfast and lunch: 2-6 (4-12/day) capsules Q96 Micronutrients or "equivalent."

And/or Chelated Lithium Orotate or Cell Salts (I feel Q96 is the most important to take because it has all the necessary neurotransmitter precursors.) Use the lithium orotate, especially if you have had success with prescription lithium, or choose to wait to buy the Q96. Buy lithium orotate at a health food store, or online.

3. An Essential Fatty Acid Supplement like fish oil, omega 3s on an empty stomach or just before bed.

4. Optional: HCL with Pepsin and/or digestive enzymes with meals.

Dietary Changes:

1. Start the day off with lemon water or salt under tongue (or salt brine).

2. Drink the correct amount of water each day at the right time away from meals.

3. Get a "salt change" to Himalayan Pink Salt. 2 tsp. per day.

4. Try to incorporate bitters into meals instead of just sweet foods. Fermented foods are also beneficial.

If you are currently on ANY medications, or just want someone live to talk with through this process, sign up for micronutrient support to safely transition from meds to med free: **www.micronutrientsupport.com**

5

How to Transition to Med Free

Holistic treatment is based on the belief that a person can't change one part of their life without changing all of it.

Julie A. Fast, Author of

Loving Someone with Bipolar Disorder

It is important to understand that there is more to the Med Free Method™ than just popping vitamins instead of prescription pills. Letting your family and doctor know that you have a plan, and a guide to ease you through the steps, can help them understand that you are serious and want their support. Here are some things that you and your support team should be aware of. After beginning lifestyle changes and implementing micronutrient (Q96) protocols, there are some things to keep in mind like:

- You may get worse before you get better.
- Lifestyle improvements may cause detox symptoms
- You probably will not be able to simultaneously take the supplements and medication indefinitely.
- There may be withdrawal symptoms as you transition off of the meds.

- Adjusting to a normal life can be much harder than most people anticipate.
- Emotionally charged events might surface that have been suppressed or numbed by medication.

There are also some physical issues that may need to be addressed first because they can interfere with the med free protocols working, some of which we have already addressed in steps one through three of the Med Free Method™. Things that can interfere with the micronutrients and other aspects of the Med Free Method™ working include:

- Digestive issues/ Candida or Yeast (Chapter 12)
- Chronic Bladder Infections (Chapter 12)
- Antibiotic Use (Take extra probiotics with natural antibiotics like oregano/olive leaf oil)
- Antacids (Use Bragg's Apple Cider Vinegar instead!)
- Lack of proper sleep and/or sleep aid use (Chapter 10)
- Poor diet (Chapter 6)
- A trip to the Dentist (Chapter 12)
- Drinking too much or too little water (Chapter 3)
- A change in exercise (Chapter 6)
- Substance abuse issues like alcohol or drug use (this chapter for help)
- Extreme Stress (Chapter 7)

If you suffer from any of these, try to work through as many of them as you can to increase your chances of success in transitioning from medications to Q96 or other supplementation.

How long does it take? "Mom! Are we there yet?"

Ask yourself: how long have you been sick? How many years have you been on medications? Or how long have you been un-medicated? Be patient with the process and realize that you can only start right where you are, and getting better is not a race, it is a process and a journey, and each person's path is different.

I have seen people notice a difference in under an hour, and I have seen people never notice anything. I have seen people come off of all medications in a week, and some who have been trying for over a year and are struggling. I wish I had a better answer, but I think honesty is best.

Because supplements do not work like drugs, you probably will not feel differently for a while. They need time to work their way into your system, replenish malnourished centers, and help your body to normalize brain operations. The brain may respond within hours, days, weeks, months, or in about approximately 10% of cases, never, so it is important to know that each person is different.

Talking to your doctor:

If you are currently on prescription medications, you will need to talk with your doctor about the importance of having a plan to slowly taper down and perhaps completely eliminate the medications. It is very dangerous to stop taking your medications right away, as most of them can have debilitating withdrawal symptoms if quit cold turkey. Almost all psychotropic drugs are addictive, despite what we may have been told.

SQUIRREL POINT

I read a brochure on bipolar that said, "The vast majority of individuals with bipolar disorder can benefit from medication. Some people worry that medication will change their personality or be addictive; neither of these beliefs is true." Doctors on their Scientific Advisory Board reviewed the brochure for accuracy. Many medications do alter personality, and most are addictive. Perhaps these doctors have not seen someone trying to come off of most anti-depressants, or Klonopin, because quitting that, even slowly, causes anxiety worse than any you had prior to taking it. My girlfriend could not even step foot out of her closet when trying to quit Klonopin. Another girl I interviewed for the book used to be a drug addict, and she said that crack was easier to forget than one of the psych meds she had been prescribed. She now is un-medicated, and swears that at least for her, bipolar is not nearly as dangerous as the drugs used to treat it.

It is important to educate yourself before talking to your doctor. When you take your supplements to your doctors to get their opinions, they will most likely tell you that they are "fine" to take along with your meds, even "good for you," but they will not believe or understand that the supplements could possibly work effectively enough to allow you to eliminate your medication. This is a dangerous assumption.

"Perhaps the main challenge in treating patients with EMPowerplus™ is managing potential interactions with conventional psychiatric medications. Although EMPowerplus™ augments the desirable effects obtained with psychiatric medications, it also increases the severity of adverse effects."[56]

If your doctor does not believe that there could be a natural solution option to your treatment protocol, or is unwilling to help you safely taper off of your medications while steadily increasing EMPowerplus™ Q96, you might have to find a new doctor if you are serious about doing this successfully. (See chapter two for how to pick a doctor) If you can't find one who will support your decision to try and heal through med free options, you will need to decide for yourself what the best treatment option is for you.

However, through "Informed Consent," doctors are supposed to be educated on "alternatives" to treating your diagnosis, as well as the risks and benefits, and should be able to effectively communicate with you the following:

1.   The patient's **diagnosis**, if known
2.   The **nature and purpose** of a proposed treatment or procedure
3.   The **risks and benefits** of a proposed treatment or procedure
4.   **Alternatives** (regardless of their cost or the extent to which the treatment options are covered by health insurance)
5.   The **risks and benefits of the alternative treatment** or procedure
6.   The risks and benefits of **not receiving** or undergoing a treatment or procedure.

If your doctors have questions on the Q96 product or drug

interactions or reduction protocols, they can call micronutrient support for the EMPowerplus™ Q96 product at: 1-888-878-3467

Unfortunately, I have seen "informed consent" violated more in psychiatry than any other medical practice.
If you continue to take the supplements along with your medications, you may make your symptoms much worse, but that is not the case for everyone.

Some people are able to do a combination of both. Just as doctors play a guessing game, using trial and error for years with your medication cocktails, you need to be prepared for some trial and error with natural products as well. There is not one thing or one dose that works the same for everyone.

When the product Q96 is working as it should, when you have gotten enough into your depleted system, your brain will begin to balance out. However, when it does, you will quickly become over-medicated, and the very prescriptions that may have been beneficial to a starving brain can cause a litany of symptoms in a normalizing brain.

Your symptoms will most likely mimic the symptoms of your disorder, causing you to think that the vitamins are not working at all and that you are getting sick or having an episode, so it is important that you educate yourself on what to expect.
"The range of beneficial response types I see with EMP range from as quickly as one to two weeks to as long as four to six months. But the most typical response pattern would be four to eight weeks. Often, the first thing that improves is irritability, rage, and agitation. Then I see cycles regulate and improve. Then I begin to see mood begin to balance and patients have fewer severe swings. After this, I begin to see anxiety issues improve." --Dr. Scott Shannon, Assistant clinical professor of child psychiatry at the University of Colorado Children's Hospital and EMPowerplus™ recommending psychiatrist. He has treated over 200 pediatric patients with EMPowerplus™.

Other than the fact that your doctor, friends, and family may all be against you trying a more natural approach to treating your mental illness (remember that they are for you being well, and are worried about a relapse or episode, but are not against you), there are several problems that can potentially arise at this stage in your recovery program:

• It is possible for bipolar symptoms to break through due to a change in treatment
• You may experience withdrawal symptoms as you reduce medications that can also mimic mental illness
• You may experience toxic "die off," as the minerals chelate (grab hold of) toxins and flush them out of your body. (This is why some children experience increased or decreased bed-wetting at this stage of the program. Toxins must be expelled, and the bladder does not want to hold onto them, so it releases them involuntarily; or the minerals can actually absorb the toxins resulting in bed wetting being stopped.)
• The very medications that helped your condition may turn on you and cause the same symptoms they were designed to treat, including, but not limited to: suicidal thoughts, racing thoughts, anxiety, nervousness, depression, and more, including physical symptoms such as sweating, upset stomach, and flu-like symptoms. The vitamins themselves cannot cause these symptoms.
• Once you start to feel better the numbing effects of the medication wear off and it may be difficult to face past memories or normal grief that may flood in.

"When I lost both my parents suddenly, I needed to get on an anti-depressant quickly just to cope. I did not even cry at their funeral, but a year later, after I had transitioned off the medication and onto just taking Q96, I had grief hit me like a train. I felt better physically and mentally without the drugs in my system, but I was not prepared for the emotional avalanche that overtook me. It is good though to be able to grieve properly for them, to heal and feel normal emotions again. I am thankful I went through the process, but it was difficult." –Susan, Idaho

Many people confuse the symptoms of medication withdrawal or over-medication with their disorder. It is important to note, however, that the micronutrients themselves do not cause any of these symptoms, and if you stick with the program, you will most likely address and heal the underlying issues of your disorder.

It is beneficial to know your medications, what side effects each has, and what withdrawal effects you might have. You can use rxlist.com for this information. The goal is to be healed naturally, and to be medication and symptom free. Keep your eye on the prize, and try not to run back to the safety of medication and the numbing of real life. When you are educated on your expectations beforehand, your chances of sticking with the med free bipolar treatment long enough for it to work will increase exponentially. After usually what takes several months of a transitional period, you can experience the health and healing that has been taking place in your body and mind all along due to the micronutrients and other steps in the Med Free Method™.

Remember that the levels and amounts of ingredients in Q96 are safe, even at the higher "loading-doses," where in the beginning I took double the amount I need now as a maintenance dose. If you trust the process, you will most likely be rewarded with a healthy brain, body, and future.

More side effects?!!

The most-commonly reported side effect of Q96 has been minor, usually temporary stomach upset, especially when taking them on an empty stomach. There is a tablet form available (also recommended for vegans) that can usually alleviate stomach upset. I have had two new Q96 users who reported that their brains were "buzzing," almost like they had bees in their brain, and the nerve-endings felt like they were tingling. I just thought this was incredibly cool evidence that the micronutrients were actually doing something, and that the ingredients were able to cross the blood-brain barrier and go to work. They both reported that the buzzing went away after the first few days and has not returned. Some people have quit or tried to quit their medications in the past and have found the symptoms of their disorder returning full-force. By simply stopping your medications, there leaves no buffer or filter between you and your disorder; but by adding the

Q96 first, well before you take your last dose of medication, you give your body and brain what it needs to stabilize functioning. The goal is to not need the medications in a couple of months, nor have the symptoms of bipolar to deal with!

Dealing with Withdrawal

Many psychiatric medications are as addictive as any other substance like tobacco, alcohol, or street drugs, but you may have no awareness of your body's or mind's dependence on them. The body can go through withdrawal for years.

After reducing or eliminating a particular prescription, you may find yourself craving it, or obsessing about it. Even many doctors are not fully aware of the side effects or withdrawal symptoms of the medications they prescribe or recommend stopping cold turkey.

It is important to find a doctor who can help you transition safely, but if not, contact:
www.micronutrientsupport.com for support.

If you are on your own, like I was when I started taking control of my disorder and its treatment, then you will need to do what is best for you as well as you can. Remember that this is not a race, and even if it takes you three, six, or twelve months to gradually become med free bipolar, I can assure you that it will be worth it. I encourage you to give it all you can, to stick with it for as long as you can, so that you may know if you are in the 80% majority for whom this treatment plan can work. The years I spent unstable and un-medicated, or deadened on meds, or struggling to find the right combinations of meds, all while dealing with the side effects and break-through bipolar symptoms, were the worst years of my life. I feel for those who, until now, have known no other options but medication, perhaps for decades.

Help with medication withdrawal or addictions

Many people with bipolar have addictions to other substances like carbohydrates, sugar (which can upset beneficial flora), chocolate, tobacco, alcohol, or street drugs, but there is natural help for overcoming these as well.

There are several things that can help overcome withdrawal symptoms and/or food cravings, including: amino acids, inositol, phosphatidyl choline, and phosphatidyl serine. Amino acids are the most commonly used remedy, however. Amino acids are one of the best tools for addictions, whether prescribed meds or otherwise, according to Julie Ross, author of The Mood Cure. She has been instrumental in helping thousands of people overcome addictions and eating disorders using diet and amino acids.

EMPowerplus™ Q96 was a great foundation to my health, but a house still needed to be built on that foundation. The Med Free Method™ is the whole building. So far we have laid the groundwork and foundation, and you may have seen dramatic improvements already in your health. Now it is time to move on to recommended nutrition guidelines.

HEALTH FOR THE *A* STUDENT WHO WANTS TO CHANGE THEIR FUTURE

6

The Med Free Diet™ for Bipolar: Mood Food

Disease enters through the mouth.

Chinese Proverb

Remember that we are the most over-fed and under-nourished nation in the world, consuming the most food containing the least amount of nutrition. Everyone has choices when it comes to food, but if you want to be and remain med free, then the diet you choose to follow could make or break your success. When we talk about which diets are best for those who are diagnosed with bipolar, we are mainly going to be addressing food for the brain and central nervous system.

Main principal: Reduce the toxins in; get the toxins out

Med Free Diet™ for Bipolar Guidelines:

    1. Only change one thing at a time. Pick something—just one thing—and do it. Make simples changes where you can. Implement one rule at a time, maybe even separated by weeks or months.

For example: if you smoke, do not tackle trying to stop right now; there are easier things you can change first that will make quitting easier and more natural when the timing is right. Maybe switch to a better brand, like Natural Native American Spirit Cigarettes, which have fewer chemicals. 66 percent of people with bipolar smoke, so if you don't, great.

If you drink alcohol to excess, make a few diet changes first or add in amino acids that can reduce alcohol, carbohydrate, or sugar cravings before trying to quit alcohol or sugar cold turkey.
Alcohol and sugar leach vitamins and minerals from the body, so if you can cut back, do. But complete depravity could only make you break down, detox too fast, or give up, especially if you are manic or depressed already.

Take things slowly, and remember that I had the advantage and disadvantage of uncovering each step in my healing spread out over many years.

Example: I recently consulted with someone who ate mostly frozen microwave dinners. His OCD made it difficult for him to cook. Making a mess in the kitchen to even cut up vegetables or thinking about meal planning would have been too overwhelming. I recommended that he give up the microwave as much as possible as it destroys the nutrients in food. Instead of reaching for the microwave entrees, he can get the frozen skillet meals that are just meat and frozen vegetables. Cooking it in one pan on the stovetop minimizes the mess. Pre-cut frozen veggies are almost as good as fresh.

Start where you are, do what you can. Do not compare where you are to others. Each of us has our own journey.

2. Focus on eating only real food. If God did not make it, don't eat it. If man messed with it, it is no longer food.
- Meats, lots of fish (avoid processed meats like lunch meats, hot dogs, etc.)
- Eggs (Free range from a local vendor is best)

- Eat Lots of healthy fats: seeds, nuts, olive oil, avocado oil, avocado, coconut oil
- Raw dairy, butter, ghee, yoghurt and cheeses when able
- Four parts vegetables to two parts fruit
- Gluten free or properly prepared grains only!
- Fermented foods unless mood sensitive (like sauerkraut, kvass, kefir, Kombucha)

3. Beware of food allergies. Many people with NBD suffer from food allergies that they actually crave. This exacerbates the condition. If you are not sure whether you are allergic, try an elimination diet for two weeks and then add in one thing at a time to see if there is a reaction. Common allergens include:

- Wheat, dairy, eggs, corn, chocolate, and pork.

4. Focus on balancing blood sugar. It is estimated that 50 percent of people with bipolar suffer from blood sugar imbalances. The body overreacts to sugary foods leading to a crash that can produce fatigue, anxiety, and irritability.

TIPS: Control amount and type of carbohydrates. Low carb diets are beneficial.

5. Eliminate all possible sugar. This is difficult today in America as almost everything in the stores contain sugar, even salad dressings and ketchup. Minerals are precious at this stage of your healing, especially magnesium. Just one molecule of sugar depletes 54 molecules of magnesium in the body.[57] Instead use:

Healthy Sweeteners in Moderation
- Grade B Maple Syrup (Not Grade A)
- Maple Sugar, Sucanat (Not turbinado!), Molasses, Sorghum
- Raw, cold-processed local honey (heating it over 175° kills the enzymes)
- Coconut Nectar, Stevia (From a South American herb, not for baking)
- Rapadura or date sugar (Occasionally)

SQUIRREL POINT

Bees understand the importance of not heating honey. They will band together and flap their wings to cool the honey. If it gets too hot they know it is now a "dead food" and will completely abandon the hive. Then we, as stupid humans, heat the honey to make it easier to extract and pour, thus depleting all of nature's hard work. When it is heated, it becomes a processed, dead food, no better really than sugar.

~~~~~~

6. Treat your food as medicine.

"Let thy food be thy medicine, and medicine be thy food."
–Hippocrates, Father of Medicine

<u>We are going the wrong way, as food used to be our primary source of medicine, and now it is the primary source of our illness.</u> Many cultures around the world still live by this food as medicine motto, and their health reflects it. Herbs and spices were used for their health benefits and not just for seasoning.

I encourage you to look into more foods as medicine each time you have an ill. I use salt for headaches instead of pills, oils for infections, onions and garlic for everything, and apple cider vinegar for acid reflux. I use spices for their anti-inflammatory and antioxidant properties. I even put cinnamon or turmeric in my coffee in the mornings along with my butter, coconut oil, honey, and raw milk.

Example: Circumin/Turmeric, the spice used in curry, is:
- Anti-inflammatory and Antioxidant
- Neuroprotective
- Neurochemical- meaning it acts in the chemical balancing of serotonin, dopamine, norepinephrine, and cortisol modulation.[58]

Mood Food: What to eat and when to eat it

Now we know WHAT to eat and WHY we should select good foods, but WHEN you eat certain things can also affect mood swings and manic/depressive episodes. Neurotransmitters are so directly affected by what we eat that the brain can respond to food in minutes. We all know what blood sugar crashes feel like, but serotonin levels, dopamine, and other mood-regulating factors are all affected by specific foods also.

I personally have found such improved health with good diet and supplementation that I do not need to worry about the details of mood food as much, but it may be helpful and I did find it quite interesting. Your body also detoxes between four AM and ten AM, so giving your digestive system a rest during these hours is a good idea.

Many nutritionists say to eat breakfast like a king, but many don't know that a big ten AM breakfast or brunch is best. I usually drink my lemon water or put Himalayan salt under my tongue right when I wake up, but then fix my coffee and two fried eggs in ghee about ten AM. When I am working and can't stick to my regular schedule, I just do the best I can and do not worry about it. Stressing about eating is just as bad as letting a few things slide.

Avoid Crashes and Mood Swings by doing these things every day:

#1: Don't Skip Meals, ever: six smaller meals help keep blood sugar level
#2: Eat regularly throughout the day
#3: Eat slowly and thoughtfully, not under stress

As a General Rule:

Many of the same foods are good for different things at different times. The same food that helps get you out of a depressed state may also get you out of a manic state. Unlike medication, your body knows what to do with nutrients and to put them where they are needed. Do not think of them as foods that will trigger mania or throw you into depression, but more of as a guide to see how your body responds to certain foods over time, and respond to your body's cravings.

Alertness Chemicals: Eating protein triggers dopamine and norepinephrine production.

Calming Chemicals: Eating complex carbohydrates can help calm mood. Proteins like turkey and milk stimulate serotonin production.

Vitamin D: is very much involved in the production of serotonin. Vitamin D is the molecule of will power and delayed gratification. Vitamin D should be taken in liquid or spray form. (See the product sources page) Decreased serotonin production can lead to inhibited creativity and the inability to follow-through with ideas. It is very important to both the depressed and the manic person to increase serotonin levels safely through foods or high quality supplements. There is an application called DMinder that can let you know when and if vitamin D is available that time of year at your elevation levels, as some states, like where I live, can't even get adequate Vitamin D from the sun during much of the year, thus making supplementation essential.

Foods to eat when depressed:
- Wild-caught fish with fins and scales
- Egg yolks (raw is best but is safest eaten from healthy farm-fresh eggs, preferably local or back-yard chickens to assure health of chicken and eggs)
- Butter (from Pasture-raised cows is important as it contains the X-factor)
- Grapefruit (not with some medications)
- Organ meats, meat fats, goose, and chicken liver
- Cod liver oil
- Caffeine (limited to 1-2 cups made with organic coffee beans in AM)
- Fish eggs and oily fish
- Fermented foods like sauerkraut
- Soaked and sprouted Nuts and Seeds
- Ancient Grains soaked and fermented (fermenting just means adding a tbsp. of yoghurt or apple-cider to the soak-

ing): Quinoa, millet, teff, amaranth, spelt, barley

Foods to Avoid when Depressed:
- Refined sugar and carbohydrates
- Alcohol

Foods to eat when Manic:
- Wild-caught fish with fins and scales
- Berries (antioxidants reduce the stress hormone cortisol which has been linked as the cause of paranoia and psychosis)
- Dark Organic Chocolate (also reduces cortisol and helps your brain produce opioids, which are "Pleasure" and "Calming" chemicals. This could reduce cravings for dangerous pleasure-seeking activities and reduce manic behaviors)
- Apples, oranges, and bananas (boost immunity and aid digestion)
- Grapefruit (high in vitamins, minerals and aids digestion. Caution with meds)
- Dairy (raw whole milk, kefir)
- Whole, properly prepared grains (help produce serotonin, calm, and satiate, as well as reduce blood sugar spikes)
- Herbal Teas (make iced or hot tea from chamomile or other calming teas)
- Lots and lots of healthy brain fats like avocado, coconut oil

Foods to Avoid when Manic:
- Caffeine
- Alcohol
- Sugar
- Processed Foods
- Fast Foods
- Lunch/processed meats
- Tyramine if sensitive (see Squirrel Point below)

SQUIRREL POINT

One common food sensitivity among many people, but especially bipolar, is an amine called Tyramine. Symptoms may include:

- *Suddenly feeling a "mad switch" after eating*
- *Mood Changes*
- *Brain Fog/fuzzy thinking*
- *Headache*
- *IBS/Diarrhea/Gas*
- *Heartburn*
- *Bad Dreams*

Foods high in Tyramine include:

- *Fermented foods like sauerkraut/cheeses and meats like salami, smoked salmon*
- *Luncheon meats*
- *Soy Sauce*
- *Tap Beer*
- *Overly ripe bananas, oranges, and avocados*

It is important to be mindful when you eat and notice unusual behavior/mood changes or signals your body gives you like acid reflux, heart burn, gas, bloating, etc.

~~~~~~

Foods that help you Sleep:

- Cheese
- Milk
- Properly prepared whole grains with a fat like butter
- Herbal teas: valerian, hope, passionflower, skullcap

Good Diets and information for the Bipolar Brain:

- #1 (but difficult to follow) by a landslide: GAPS Diet™ by Dr. Natasha Campbell-McBride: www.gaps.me
- Ketogenic Diet (especially helpful for bipolar and seizures)
- The Japanese Diet/ The Okinawa diet plan
- The Maker's Diet and Beyond Organic by Jordan Rubin
- Med Free Diet™ & Cookbook (upcoming book for com-

plete brain diet guidelines, Spring, 2014)
- Paleo Diet
- Anti-inflammatory diets
- Gluten-free Diet and properly prepared grains
- Low-carb diet or Specific Carb Diet (with adjustments)
- Atkins (with adjustments)
- Nourishing Traditions (best cookbook) by Sally Fallon
- Weston-Price Foundation: www.westonaprice.org
- Price-Pottenger Nutrition Foundation www.ppnf.org

Dangerous Diets for the Brain:

What about the diet crazes, or should we say "crazies"? Remember that people with NBD are usually the most compromised nutritionally, but also need foods that are easy to digest and assimilate nutrients from while their gut and brains heal. There may be a time when you can eat any food on any menu, or follow whatever diet you want, but for now keep in mind that our goal is to be well, whole, and free of medications and hospitalizations. Forget other theories on eating and diet for now, but revisit ones that may be important to you later when you are well enough to do them correctly. The diets below that probably will not serve your brain or your healing, at least for now.

Low Fat Diets Starve the Brain

Your brain is 80 percent fat…it is essential that we, as a people with brain deficiencies (and everyone with a brain), eat fat! Many people have started to wake up to the fact that you can actually eat fat to lose fat, as talked about in the groundbreaking book by the same name, written by Dr. Mary Enig and Sally Fallon. The brain is mostly fat. Cholesterol has been painted out as a villain, while sugar is touted as "sweet and innocent" compared to artificial sweeteners. The cholesterol heart myth has been purported way too long, and the food industry has made a killing, BY killing people with preposterous information. For more information on the "cholesterol myth", read *The Great Cholesterol Myth* by Dr. Stephen Sinatra.

Pop butter pills instead of cholesterol-lowering drugs, and be amazed at the health difference for your brain *and* your heart. Who knew that eating bacon and eggs cooked in butter was better for you than low-fat milk and cereal! Now you do.

You will need a lot of high-quality fats to heal the blood-brain barrier, renew neuron pathways, build new tissue, and repair gut, heart, and cell damage. If the brain has not been getting fed, then other organs have also not been getting fed properly.

Anorexia Nervosa and bulimia are also forms of mental illness that are very difficult to treat, because the very fats that will correct the distorted self-image are the same ones the person is most afraid of. Overcome your fear of healthy fat, and you will lose weight and your brain will begin to heal.

"I have no doubt that the fashion for vegetarian and vegan diets is a major cause of mental illness in our young people."
--Dr. Natasha Campbell-McBride

Vegetarianism/Veganism's Health Myth

People who embrace a plant-based diet are sometimes healthier than people who eat meat, mostly because they tend to eat a "cleaner" diet overall, with less processed, refined foods, but people groups who eat healthy meats, dairy and a variety of plant-based foods are the healthiest and most disease free of all, given they are not allergic to a certain food, according to Dr. Weston A. Price, a dentist who traveled the world studying nutrition and corresponding health in indigenous people groups.

It is almost impossible to get all of your nutritional requirements, especially to feed the brain adequately, from a vegetarian diet, and even more difficult from a vegan diet. "Vegetarian diets have been touted as 'healthy' and 'planet saving' for decades. Every one of these statements is not only wrong, but down-right deceptive."[59] I recommend every parent whose child is considering vegetarianism to have them read The Vegetarian Myth by Lierre Keith and do a book report on it before agreeing to let them.

People with "brain symptoms" especially may need a wider variety of foods. We are omnivores, not herbivores, and our needs for nutritional health reflects an omnivorous diet consisting of high-quality proteins from meats, fish, and eggs. Most animals that eat plants have two stomachs to digest them. Plant proteins are harder to digest, especially when the gut is already compromised and enzymes that break down plant fiber may be low. Humans lack the enzyme cellulase, which is necessary for digesting plant fibers, making purely vegetarian, vegan, or raw food diets difficult for the body to sustain over time. The nutrients are harder to assimilate from plants, so supplementation is especially important for coming back around from a plant-based diet.

Hydrochloric acid is unique to meat-eaters, and is primarily meant to help digest meat. Our variety of digestive enzymes, manufactured by the pancreas, is designed for breaking down both plants and animal matter.[60] Remember that most people, especially with bipolar, are deficient in HCL due to salt-restricted diets or poor-quality salt, so Himalayan Pink Salt is essential for life, digestion, and health.

If you know your body well and can do a safe vegetarian diet, then of course that is your choice. There should never be any judgment from anyone!

"If my books piss a lot of people off but make them think, then I have succeeded."
–Aspen L. Morrow

7

Toxins out:
Clean the Fish Tank

There are nationwide and local epidemiological studies showing that when {air pollution} goes up, premature deaths go up.

Matthew Lakin, PhD, U.S. Environmental Protection Agency

Oh the irony of the EPA. The Environmental Protection Agency (EPA) has not banned a chemical in the US in seventeen years. It has only issued regulations on nine chemicals, out of over 80 thousand![61] That is why we must take our health into our own hands. Your doctor won't do it, and neither will the government.

Remember the analogy about the fish tank? How can we expect to heal when our already overloaded system must also contend with filtering out 85,000 toxic substances? Working on cleaning up our diet, supplementing it with detoxing minerals, but then putting our body back into a toxic environment is like giving a fish a bath and then throwing it back in a dirty fish tank.

Besides, cleaning up your environment, inside and out can help you heal faster. We live in a very toxic world and need to pay attention to what goes on our skin, in our mouths, what we breathe in, and what we wash our bodies and clothes with. If this step is too much to think about for now, then come back to it in a few months or even years, but remember that your body's natural detoxification system, found primarily in the gut, is already over-loaded, and adding more can short-circuit the system. Just like all living things, air quality, water quality, and a toxin-free environment are important to thrive.

Step Four: Detox & Exercise by Accident
Clean the outside of your "fish tank"

Head, Shoulders, Knees, and Toes:

Your skin is your largest organ. What you put on your skin you absorb straight into your bloodstream. You would be better off drinking some of the toxins we use around the house (so your liver could filter it first), than to put in on topically.[62]

For your Body: shampoos, conditioners, body washes, and shaving creams are a necessity, but look for ones that do not contain parabens, formaldehyde, or sodium lauryl (laureth) sulfate.
For your face: Makeup ingredients for skin and eyes are also important. Bioceutica is a company that uses coconut water-based skincare and gluten-free makeup.

Feminine Products also have a lot of chemicals in them. Look for "organic" options next time you are in a health food store. Sunscreens should be mineral-based with as few ingredients as possible. Zinc oxide and titanium dioxide are the ones to look for. Lose the sunscreen for the first twenty minutes in favor of acquiring vitamin D, but then apply sunscreen. According to Arthur W. Perry, MD, FACS, most ingredients in our sunscreen are endocrine disruptors that can interfere with the normal function of hormones: thyroid, estrogen, testosterone, and progesterone.[63]

For your home: Cleaning products for your home should be free of toxins and should be able to be used without gloves. Dishwasher detergents leave behind residue that you eat, and some of the ingredients can build up in tissues and are stored for years. Many direct sales companies like Melaleuca, Healthy Home, and Bioceutica are ingredient conscious. Seventh Generation and others can be purchased at stores like Fred Meyer.

Better yet, make your own. Here are the top basic ingredients to clean almost everything in your home: DIY Cleaning:

- White Vinegar, Hydrogen peroxide
- Borax, baking soda
- Essential oils: tea tree, lavender, lemongrass or eucalyptus
- Castile soap (like Dr. Bronner's Magic Soap)
- Fresh herbs, citrus, or citrus peels
- Olive or vegetable oil
- Water, salt (Use all that bad table salt you have!)

There are three eventual must-have products for the home that I recommend, all from the same company: Vollara (see product section in back of book).

Air: The air inside your house is more polluted than outside. Open windows when you can, get filters, and use an air purifier. Some of the most amazing technology I have seen to date is the FreshAir Surround by Vollara. It uses the same ozone science as nature, destroys odors, eliminates smoke and reduces harmful contaminants. It can even sterilize surfaces like bathrooms or deodorize clothes thrown on top of it. We have reduced how often we get sick, and how often we clean the bathrooms!

Water: There are entire books about water, and I covered how much water to drink in Chapter Three, but drinking the right kind of water is important also. Water is mostly what we are made of, so water that will help buffer acid, help remove toxins, and is easily absorbed by your body can help do double duty alongside your other health improvements. Ionized alkaline water also has antioxidant properties and proper pH levels. The LivingWater unit achieves all of these, but Kangen water machines are also exceptional, although more expensive. Reverse Osmosis units remove all the good and bad in the water, but are great filters.

Laundry: I bought a Laundry Pure unit from Vollara to reduce the amount of detergent I use in the wash. I don't fully understand how it works, but I love it. I even use the water from my washing machine to clean my carpets and floors as it is oxidized and cleans without chemicals. It attaches above my washing machine and just re-routes my hoses through it.

Swimming: Avoid chlorinated pools as much as possible. Instead, swim in salt-based or saline swimming pools or natural waters.

I have had two friends who found out they actually had mold in their brain wreaking havoc on their health, moods, and energy! One is writing a book on how her health improved by just getting rid of the toxins in her home. It is stories like hers that make me try to do what I can to eliminate the toxins in my environment.

For your yard: Use organic weed control like straight vinegar on weeds (not in flower beds), and safe fertilizers on your lawn. Organic pest control in and outside of the house is important also, as these are some of the harshest chemicals you can be exposed to. Ten years ago even thinking about toxins and their impact on my mental health was not something I was ready or capable to do when I was still sick. At that time in my life cleaning a dozen dirty baby bottles was a daunting task for quite a while. We did not have a dishwasher at the time, and I did not function well as one either.

Remember to accept yourself where you are now, without judgment. However, making one small change at a time can make a huge impact over time. I recommend replacing household and toiletry items one by one with something healthier as they run out, unless you are able to throw them out to buy new. I replaced mine over time. Being on food stamps and public housing and unable to work, I couldn't just up and throw out all of our household cleaners, toiletries, and feminine products.

Toxic People: If you have toxic or negative people in your life, consider ending the relationship, asking them to treat you better, or limit the amount of time you spend with them. If *you* are that toxic person, read Chapter Nine.

Spring Clean Your Body: Detox Your Insides: Everyone is a little bit toxic because we live in a toxic world. Since most of us have digestive issues, as well as a litany of other health issues, getting the toxic sludge out of our engines will help it run smoother and help the other steps work more effectively. But the good news is that each of the five steps in the Med Free Method™ are doing this very thing all along the way, so focusing on it may not even be as necessary as it is for other people who aren't doing the other recommendations.

We have an amazing filtration system more complex than anything on earth, but it needs to be reset on a regular basis. Here are just a few suggestions, but talk to your new health practitioner (Chapter Two) or get a naturopath who knows even more about this than I do.

- Detox your colon
- Detox your liver
- Detox your kidneys

Don't ever use chelating drugs. They cause all sorts of damage. Detoxing and even taking mineral supplements can make psychiatric symptoms worse for a time; as they flush toxins out of the system they can flare up the systems. Push through it if you are using naturally healthy ways to detox. Don't give up half way through!

1. Change your diet: Eat more fiber-rich fruit and vegetables. Smoothing and juicing can be a great way to increase nutrients without changing a lot of things at once. Add fresh ginger or beets for increased benefit. Black elderberry is one of nature's most potent natural detoxifiers.

2. Use natural colon-cleansing supplements like "Dr. Nuzum's (see book's afterword) Digest Detox." His special blend is a gentle digestive detoxification formula that enables you to eliminate excess waste and abdominal bloating. It contains: slippery elm, cascara sagrada, and more and is powerful but gentle.

3. Use an enema at home to irrigate your colon. Coffee enemas are highly touted in some circles. Colonics clinics are an option also, but can be expensive.

4. Soak for twenty minutes in a warm herbal/mineral bath. Help draw out toxins by infusing your bath water with eucalyptus, wintergreen, peppermint, fennel, cinnamon, and especially magnesium and Epsom salts.

5. Find some natural hot springs. As part of the Japanese cul-

ture, they regularly detox in Onsens, natural mineral baths which are scattered all over the country. Many of them are co-ed and publicly nude bathing houses. I sure got some stares though as a foreign white chick when I went to the females only Onsen in Fukuoka, Japan. They had never seen a white blue-eyed "gaijin" join them. Hey, "when in Rome".... Now that we live back in Idaho, we regularly frequent many of the mineral and lithium-rich hot springs that are within a short driving distance, as well as explore new ones almost every summer.

Explore hot springs that are especially high in lithium content, as this can exponentially increase the benefits of soaking in hot springs. Even just inhaling the steam, especially when it is high in sulfur. Hot springs are reputed to also help alleviate the following conditions:

- Skin diseases, acne, eczema
- Women's diseases, PMS, peri/menopause, etc.
- Asthma, neuralgia, arteriosclerosis, rheumatism
- Shoulder, neck and wrist pains. They also have a detoxifying and mucolytic effect of clearing mucus from the lungs
- Digestive issues

Garlic is known as a great healing herb, but mostly because of the sulfur it contains.

8

Exercise on Accident
(Cause it's Overated Anyway)

Only exercise and eat healthy on days you want to be happy. .

Unknown

I encourage you to exercise on accident...on purpose. We have all heard to "park further away from the door," or "take the stairs instead of elevator," but you might need some help thinking of other ways to exercise on accident.

Don't stress about exercise so much. According to Campbell-McBride, Americans are obsessed with exercise way too much. Most of the rest of the world are quite the couch potatoes, and most are healthier than us if they eat better. When I heard that, I thought: So if most people around the world don't go to the gym, why should I? Possibly unrelated to each other, but obesity rates, *and* gym memberships have doubled in the past thirty years. What we are doing isn't working.

I always want to know why I should do something, and what is in it for me if I do? Good nutrition and supplementation are far more important than exercise, so if you cannot afford good food, supplements, and your gym membership, cancel the gym membership. Exercise is important, but it is the movement that is the most beneficial. However, I am not your doctor, or your personal trainer (both of whom probably don't like me right now), so don't just take my word for it.

With that being said, however, I will discuss why movement is important, and why you can do it.

Exercising stirs the waters.

I used to hike in the Idaho mountains alone. I would leave our family campground at sunrise and intentionally get lost for the day, climbing higher and higher with the sun. I took water tablets with me so I could drink fresh, mountain stream water, once purified. I followed serpentine creek switchbacks hoping to lunch beside the lake source. Instead of a pristine mountain lake, one day I came upon a large stagnant pond. Decomposing leaves muddied the water and emitted decaying gases and smells, moss collected like Jupiter's rings around the bank and had spread like a mucous-filled cold. I could almost see the bacteria and West Nile viruses brewing in the pond's cauldron.

The stagnant water was teaming with undesirables: thick mosquitos and flies welcomed my living presence, swarming me as if to consume me all at once. Death is attracted to life. But what happens if fresh water flows into and out of that pond? The water quickly clears up, cleans up, and the undesirables leave to find a new home.

Putrefied water is what we have inside our bodies when we do not exercise. Toxins from the daily exposures to pollution, herbicides, insecticides, and a litany of food chemicals gather in our bodies. Bad bacteria and parasites are allowed free reign of the toxic sludge pooling up inside our bodies, tissues, organs, and cells like pond water. We need to stir the waters. Since we are made mostly of water, we need to be a stream of living water, not a stagnant puddle.

Think of what happens when water sits for a long time in a cup, puddle, or pond. It eventually gets covered with slime and gunk, breeds disease, and becomes toxic…. That process is similar to what's going on in many people's bodies. On the other hand, when water moves, life thrives…. That's a perfect picture of what exercise does.[64]

We have talked about how important elimination is; just as trapped water stagnation can be stirred up by proper soil drainage or a moving water source, when we get our drainage system, our bowels, working, drink more water, and then shake it all up with a little movement, miraculous health can happen. The toxins that we bring in: pollution, processed foods, chemicals from body and cleaning products, pesticides on food, mercury from tooth fillings, and chlorine and fluoride in tap water, can be handled and eliminated from our body better.

Exercise = anti-depressants

Exercise has been found as effective, and sometimes more effective, than anti-depressants for mental health. It also reduces risk of Alzheimer's by fifty percent, and anxiety by forty-five percent. I firmly believe that it was my extensive exercise schedule that helped me ward off many symptoms of my bipolar in high school.

The best exercise for the least amount of work

Since I had run track for so many years, I figured that I had fit in a whole lifetime of exercise and didn't need to work out ever again. Apparently it does not work that way. At age twenty-four I weighed 220 pounds. Some of it was left over psych-med weight-gain, then baby weight, then marriage weight, poor eating, on top of no exercise. The final nail, thirty pounds of nails, was a birth-control shot in the arm that was the hardest weight to lose of all.

I would like to be able to tell you that I found the motivation to put my running shoes back on and lose the weight, but I didn't. I did everything the slow and easy, lazy way, as usual. "If it ain't easy, I ain't doin' it," has been my mantra and will be the theme of my cookbook, as I don't even really like to cook! Until I found a lazy way to exercise I did not do that either.

So how do you exercise and be lazy at the same time? And no, I am not talking about curling weights in a recliner or wearing one of those vibrating belts: I am talking about rebounding.

Rebounding or using a Cellerciser®: The fancy words for jumping on a trampoline (If purchading a Cellerciser®, please do so from your QSciences independent business owner or from the resources link at the back of the book)

What if you had access to gasoline that was about seventy percent more effective for a lot less cost? That is what rebounding is compared to almost every other form of exercise! According to NASA report findings, rebounding is almost 70% more effective for less cost of oxygen, energy output (metabolic cost), and time spent necessary to achieve results![65]

Rebounding is one of the most effective exercises in existence. It requires simply a mini-trampoline ($5 at a thrift store, $25 at Wal-Mart, or fancy ones for up to $2,000. For the difference in quality and for less back and knee strain, the Cellerciser® is only $350.00US) or a backyard trampoline. Just ten minutes spent jumping on a trampoline is equivalent to thirty or more minutes of any other exercise.

There are now more expensive machines, like the vibrational exercise machines that mimic rebounding, and can deliver sixty minutes worth of running benefits in just ten minutes. A good vibrational exercise machine for personal use costs about $2-$3000, but commercial ones can exceed $15,000. If you were to join a gym, look for one that already has vibration machines as a part of their equipment inventory.

But for the person who just wants to keep it simple, rebounding on a mini-trampoline offers most of the benefits of vibration machines at home for a fraction of the cost. I highly recommend rebounding at home three to five times per week for just ten to thirty minutes at a time. I like to do ten minutes, three days per week unless I am feeling more ambitious, which is not very often. That's it. Done. If you have access to a vibration exercise machine, just ten minutes, three to five times per week can deliver even better health results.

According to Albert E. Carter, and Dr. Morton Walker, there are at least thirty-three ways your body benefits from rebounding. Here are just some of the benefits:

1. Protects joints from the chronic fatigue and impact delivered compared to exercising on hard surfaces. (Esp. the Cellerciser®)
2. Benefits lymphatic circulation, stimulating the body's immune capacity for fighting current disease, destroying cancer cells, eliminating antigens, and preventing future illness.
3. Circulates more oxygen to the tissues, cells, and brain. This increases nutrient delivery to the brain and organs!
4. Helps the body detox at the physical and cellular level.
5. Provides an increased G-force (gravitational pull), which strengthens the musculoskeletal systems.
6. Improves resting metabolic rate so that more calories are burned for hours after exercise.
7. Strengthens the heart and other muscles and organs, including the brain, so that they work more efficiently.
8. Improves the brain's responsiveness, balance, coordination, and reduces clumsiness (dyspraxia).
9. Can offer relief from neck and back pains, headaches, and other pain caused by lack of exercise. Rebound exercise has been shown to benefit body alignment and posture.
10. Enhances digestion and elimination processes.
11. Allows for deeper and easier relaxation and sleep.
12. Results in better mental performance, with keener learning processes.[66]

Other than being vitally important to getting our fluids moving in our body so that we are not a stagnant pond, for me, rebounding is fun. I find it is difficult to stay or get depressed when I make myself go jump on a trampoline while listening to Katy Perry's "Firework" to start my day. We just purchased an outdoor trampoline for our children; it has been a great way to spend some quality time with them while benefitting us emotionally, physically, and mentally.

For indoor use, a good, mid-priced option that is more effective than the lower-grade rebounders is the Cellerciser® by David Hall. See the product resources section in the back of the book on where to get special pricing for this incredible piece of workout equipment or the person who gave you this book if they are a QSciences idependent business owner.

Other accidental ways to exercise: Although you may not have jumped on a trampoline "by accident" since you've become an adult, it is an "accidental" way that children love to exercise instinctively. Here are some "grown-up" ways to fit in exercise without joining a gym. Becoming like a kid again is not a bad thing.

- Visit a waterpark. I promise you will walk a lot and climb a lot of stairs. (Even if you don't have kids, tag along with a friend or take your nephews or niece)
- Park further away
- Walk to the store, or somewhere, or nowhere
- Tour a vineyard
- Learn to ballroom dance: many communities have free lessons and cheap dances, often with great live music, to stay for after the free lesson. Ballroom dancing with my grandfather is one of my fondest memories of him, and it kept he and my grandma close. Now he dances with the residents at his nursing home; he has always been the life at any party.
- Try belly-dancing, or other dance classes
- Take the stairs over the elevator
- Golf without a cart
- Dance or skip in a store (Try it and enjoy the stares!)
- Fidget (It burns up to 350 calories/day!)
- Always walk fast
- Laugh: it exercises your diaphragm and burns calories, all while increasing endorphins.
- Chin up, straighten up, and suck it in: Good posture attracts opportunities, uplifts mood, looks better, and increases muscle tone.
- Walk and talk: If you are on the phone, lap around the

living room or yard.
- Enjoy nature. Drive to a greenbelt, foothills, park, garden, hike, camp, canoe, water ski, or white-water raft.
- Cook your meals; meal planning involves shopping, prep, and cleanup. It is healthier and gets you moving a lot more than the drive-through.
- If married, step it up in the bedroom.
- Garden. This scared me, still does, and I thought it was something I could not do, but playing in the dirt is not only great for getting soil-based-organisms (SBOs), but is also good for food, exercise, mental clarity, a sense of accomplishment, and mental health.

Notice there were no weights involved, no stretches, squats or sit-ups. There was no treadmill or fancy running shoes, no laps around the track, no Zumba steps. This is how you can exercise on accident, just by getting involved in a hobby or life. It is the best exercise for both your body and mind.

A Word of Caution about Exercise
Caution #1: Obviously you should talk to your doctor about starting an exercise routine, but of equal concern is the additional complications for people with mental health issues, especially anyone who is on, or has ever been on, psychiatric medications. Medications can be stored in fatty tissues, and exercising can release them into the blood stream, causing sudden side effects or symptoms mimicking the disorder. If you are aware of this then you are less likely to be blind-sided by it if it happens to you. Remember that exercise can be a powerful way to detox, so do not be afraid of this happening, as the goal is eventually work all of the medication out of all your systems, tissues, and organs.

"You were bought at a price, therefore glorify God in your body and your spirit, which is God's!"
1 Corinthians 6:20

Caution #2: Exercise Creates Expensive Sweat!

Don't sweat out all of your supplementation: high performance athletes do not live as long as the average couch potato, and have more bone and joint problems.[67] This is caused in part by the huge amounts of sweat excreted over a lifetime. Sweat is comprised of lot more than just water. Sweat releases toxins like ammonia and urea, but also releases important nutrients, minerals, electrolytes, and salt. Just like drinking too much water can dilute the minerals your brain needs to function, over-exercising can also. If you exercise more than a couple hours total per week, be sure and replace not just the water, but take extra micronutrients and good salt. Salt tablets and water were regularly given to men who worked out in the sun all day for good reason!

FOR THE GRADUATE STUDENT WHO WANTS **ZERO** SYMPTOMS

9

Mental Mindset Recovery™:
Surviving Bipolar PTSD

Enter every activity without giving mental recognition to the possibility of defeat. Concentrate on your strengths, instead of your weaknesses... on your powers, instead of your problems."

Paul J. Meyer

Mental illness is a debilitating disorder, but it affects more than just the physical, biological parts of the brain. It affects you emotionally, spiritually, and psychosocially. Believing that you can recover from mental illness is well established as an important part of actually being able to heal, but the affects of past traumas and damaged relationships cannot heal by just supplementing and changing your diet!

Step Five is: Mental Mindset Recovery™

In 2006, my physical mind had been healed for about three years. There were no actual debilitating symptoms of bipolar. I could read again, write again, even laugh again. My marriage was good, and I loved being a mom. We had moved to Idaho from Oklahoma, and purchased our first home. My son was almost four, and God had answered my hearts' desire and had given me the baby daughter of my dreams.

My life on the outside looked perfect, but inside my mind was still broken from mental illness. The words of that doctor reverberated inside my head until I had done more than just believe them: I had become them. "You will be on meds the rest of your life; you may have trouble keeping a job…" I had beaten the med thing and had children successfully without postpartum depression or psychosis, despite his warning, but I kept waiting for the ball to drop.

I did not think I could keep a job or go back to work outside of the home. Even though the damage in my brain had healed and it was functioning properly, my mindset was still sick. My mind was still broken on an emotional level, despite my brain functioning fine on a physical level! But how do you get out of a prison of your own making?

When people start to get well, there are still many things other than the physical symptoms yet to overcome. People often think that becoming medication free with a mental illness is as simple as replacing a prescription pill with a supplement. If only it were that easy. The medications usually numb real life, and when that numbing is gone, there can be a lot of pain that comes up. It might be an easy transition for a blessed few, but here are some of the things that may come up for most people:

- Feeling regret for the years your disorder stole.
- Remembering stuff you, or others, did while sick.
- Seeing things you did while ill in a new light.
- Recalling things you couldn't remember before, or people telling you of things.
- Feeling guilty for things that you did
- Having difficulty forgiving others or them forgiving you or focusing on the past
- Others still treating you like you are ill or not being supportive of journey
- Mourning the death of a loved one whom you couldn't

properly grieve sick
- Wondering what to do now with your life
- Having trouble controlling negative thought patterns
- Breaking habits that arose from your illness
- Finding new coping skills for difficult situations
- Being tempted to drink or do drugs to be numbed again or relapsing suddenly and not knowing why

Things that can help heal your Mindset:

1.   **Believe you are well, or will be soon.** Believing that you can recover from any illness is well established as an important part of actually being able to heal. Research has proved that people of faith are more likely to recover from chronic illness. People who believe they will get better heal faster and sometimes befuddle the doctors. An article in Psychology Today even acknowledges it may not just be the placebo effect.[68] Hopefully by now you believe you can recover. However, if you don't, it is something that can be worked on.

"And all things, whatsoever ye shall ask in prayer, *believing*, ye shall receive." –Matthew 21:22 (KJV)

2.   **Know that you are not alone, nor are you an alien.** Whatever you are feeling, or how alone you feel, there are people who understand and have been there before. Find someone to talk to who understands without judgment.

SQUIRREL POINT

There are a few support groups for people who have recovered from mental illness. I never have joined a support group, because I no longer feel like I fit in with people who struggle with bipolar. Most of the talk was about symptoms, past behaviors, failed relationships, and medication changes. I don't suffer anymore, and I want others to enjoy the kind of health and healing that they may never have thought possible. Surround yourself with people like who you want to become, who believe full and complete recovery is possible and even likely. An expected outlook of wellness is highly preferable to a group of people who never have the intention or hope of recovery. If you don't want to be sick, then stop being around sick people. Stop listening to people who say this disorder is an incurable, life-long condition that can only be treated with medication.

~~~~~~

3.   **Things "you" did while ill were not really you.** Bipolar sometimes feels like we have multiple personalities, but instead of being able to retreat into un-consciousness while our evil twin or alter ego comes out to fight our battles, we get to experience the things we could not stop ourselves from doing or saying, even if we cannot always remember the details. Sometimes it was like watching myself in either slow motion or high speed, but power-less to stop the next frame. Other times details came back to me years later, like seeing part of a movie I had missed the first time cause I stepped out to use the restroom. It is weird to feel like you were absent for part of your life. Remembering parts that you have forgotten or buried can be worse than going through it the first time.

4.   **Let the memories come.** Mourn, cry, rage, whatever you need to, but then let them go. The brain is a scary realm, but just like a person who has a seizure cannot help drooling or thrashing, you did not have full control over your actions either. If your emotions and feelings were distorted because of the illness or medications, know that this is normal. You may need to take time now to grieve for the loss of a loved one or lost opportunity. It is usual for a flood of emotions to break through a dam that has held them back, sometimes for decades.

5.   **Take responsibility for what happened or mistakes that were made.** Try to make amends with people even if you shouldn't have to apologize or explain something that they could never fully understand. Pay back debts that were racked up in manic or even depressed states, knowing that you took the high

road even if what you did was out of your complete control. I destroyed my credit in the years of manic episodes I had between ages 19-22, and that took seven years to recover from, but now I am so proud of how far I have come on my own. Make it right as best you can, then let it go. Consider the overspending an investment in your learning, or treat it like a medical bill that was unavoidable.

6.   **Forgive yourself and others.** Your illness was not your fault. It is also difficult for other people to know how to act around you. Forgive yourself even the most horrendous acts, knowing that was not the REAL you, the healthy you: the you who is becoming well. Forgive others, whatever they did, even if it is seemingly unforgivable. God will judge them; please don't carry that burden. When my sister and I both experienced guys who took advantage of us during manic episodes, it would be easy to be angry for putting ourselves in those situations and hate the perpetrators, but that does not serve our future. Forgive others so that you may also be forgiven. Forgive so that you can be healed. Harboring un-forgiveness can rot your insides and keep you ill. Let it go and go grow.

Tips for Creating a New Life

> **"Cast all your anxiety on Him because He cares for you."**
> **1 Peter 5:7 (NIV)**

Change your words – Watch what you are saying to yourself and to others. Don't tell yourself that you are sick, worthless, and capable of nothing. I believe that you are created the same way now as when the Creator, El Shaddai, knit you together in your mother's womb. You are fearfully and wonderfully made. God gave you a sound mind (II Timothy 1:7) and a hope and a future (Jeremiah 29:11). He has already given us the cure that came from the very earth HE SPOKE into existence – from the very dust of the earth that formed us. This is what I believe; you get to choose what you believe.

Words are so powerful that they have the energy to CREATE. We are created in His image, and although we are not God, nor will we become a god (Satan's lie in the garden), we have power and dominion over His creation by the words we speak. Whatever you believe is your choice, but when you start paying attention to your words, you can feel the change taking place in your body on a cellular level. I know it is extremely difficult sometimes to control your thoughts and words, more difficult than for most, but small changes can make a big difference.

Your words and thoughts create your reality.

Instead of: "I can't afford that"
Choose: "How can I afford that?" or
"I choose not to spend my money on that."
Instead of: "I am worthless"
Choose: "How can I bring more value?"
Instead of: "I am broke."
Choose: "What can I do to make more money?"
Instead of: "I can't afford to give up my disability, or food stamps, or Medicaid..."
Choose: "I am no longer able to qualify because I make too much money and I am so proud of how far I have come!"

Change your thoughts – Believe me when I say I know that it is impossible to just 'snap out of it', or just 'get over' negative thoughts. Some people can. Good for them. "Just change your thinking and you will change your life" kind of statements used to make my blood boil, as if it were possible to just think my way well to recover from my bipolar. People have said to me, "You have 'attracted' everything you have into your life by the thoughts you think." True, in some regards, but harsh when it comes to a disorder or illness that you were born with! Did I attract bipolar and the negative, dark suicidal thoughts that accompanied it?

So if your thoughts are the one thing you have never seemed to have any control over, what hope do you have?

I had, and still have, an uphill battle when it comes to controlling what I think about or what I say in response to things. I once made the mistake of saying "I can't" in front of a personal development trainer. His words in response were certainly harsher than my use of the word "can't". He told me I was toxic and that I should just go sit at a different table and to stay away from his team. Wow! He was someone I looked up to, and his words stung me to the core. For people recovering from a brain disorder, that is easier said than done.

"What you think about you bring about." –The Secret

I understand that this is an especially difficult thing I am asking of you, but changing your thoughts really can make an impact on yourself, your loved ones, and your working relationships. Be proud of every single thought that you can get control of, knowing that our disability makes it all the more impressive when you finally do.

At first I found it easier to start with changing my words than my thoughts. Even though my brain does not race as much, act up, or act out like it used to, thoughts are still sometimes difficult to reign in. Words have become easier however.

You can change your thoughts and emotions immediately by thinking of something joyful, or something you are grateful for, singing a song, or remembering a happy experience.

Try to focus on the good, not the bad. Instead of thinking of all the bad things in my past, I focus on something I am grateful for today, even if it is just to be thankful I have two eyes and two ears. There is always someone worse off than you.

SQUIRREL POINT

Reading five to ten pages of a good "self help" book everyday can help turn around negative thoughts and put you on a steady path in the right direction.

Great Books I recommend:
I Inherited a Fortune, by Paul J. Meyer

If You Think You Can, by TJ Hoisington
Unlock Your Legacy: 25 Keys for Success, by Paul J Meyer*
*Paul J Meyer's work inspired Zig Ziglar and John C Maxwell and impacted millions of lives.

~~~~~~

Change your View – Visualize what you want your future to look like. Begin imagining a different life. Dream again. Quit watching TV.

I started out in my recovery with a very bad attitude, and would watch Wheel of Fortune every night. Sitting on the couch, eating Hamburger Helper, I would sit there and get mad at the people smiling, laughing, and winning exotic trips. I told myself every day that the only way I would ever get to go somewhere like that was if I were lucky enough to win a trip off of WOF! For the next few years I took the time to change my lottery mentality. I am glad I did, or I would still be sitting on that couch every night promptly at 6:30pm.

Fix the biochemical brain imbalances with supplementation, diet, and exercise; and then work on the mindset. Getting the brain chemistry balanced first makes controlling thoughts and directing dreams easier! Look to the future instead of the past. Create a dream board and put up pictures of things you would like to do. Look ahead, not back. Pick out a place you would like to travel to and hang up a picture of it.

This tactic, along with a good attitude and hard work, helped me earn four all-expense-paid trips to the Dominican Republic, Cancun twice, and Hawaii with my business. I did not win them off of Wheel of Fortune! Changing my view with a poster helped me literally change my view. My husband and I had never been able to take a honeymoon, and I was so grateful to be able to repay him just a little for all the years he worked so hard to support our family while I was sick.

Be aware of "Bipolar PTSD" – Breaking bad habits can be hard. Whether it is the habit of yelling at your children because your mom yelled at you, or quitting smoking, habits can come out of almost anything, but especially a mental illness.

132

An acquaintance of mine, Autumn Stringam, talked about how before she had recovered from bipolar she would flap her hands against her head repeatedly as a coping strategy, but then found that she still did it every now and then for a while after she was better. What had begun in mental illness carried over as a bad habit. She has now been able to free herself of the mental illness and all of its bad habits, but it took time.

Natural remedies or even medications don't do all the work for you, and there may be residual effects of illness, habits, or behaviors for a long time that you may need to work on correcting. This does not mean you are still mentally ill; it just means that you have been through a very real ordeal. And, just like a soldier experiencing posttraumatic stress after combat, you may have some bipolar PTSD.

Be patient with yourself and remember we are all works in progress. I was somewhat of a cutter, but the one time I really lost it (to prove a point no-less, not to kill myself), I cut my arm five times, all the way to the bone! I get to carry those scars the rest of my life and try and explain them to my children and professional strangers over coffee when they ask. I would be lying if I said I never feel ashamed of them, but they are part of my bipolar PTSD, and I can choose to look at them with shame and embarrassment, or forgive myself and wear them as a badge of courage for the battle scars they are. Having bipolar can be as devastating as coming through a war, commend yourself that you are here, alive, and wanting to find a way through to safety, peace, and freedom.

> **"Whatever you vividly imagine, ardently desire, sincerely believe, and enthusiastically act upon... must inevitbly ome to pass!" --Paul J. Meyer**

Look on the Bright Side – The whole world is yours! Even my four year old knows that the whole world was created just for her. When she sees a shooting star while camping, or a sunset, she exclaims: look mom, God did that just for ME! Children know how to dream and talk to themselves positively!

The universe was created just for you as well. You own

every sunrise, every sunset, and every star in the sky. All you have to do is take it, claim it, and enjoy it. There is more evidence of abundance than lack in creation. Look at the stars, the sands, the water, and even our bodies: you could see with one eye, yet you have two, two arms, two legs, and more than you need, just in case. If someone were to strip you of even your arms and legs you would still be able to accomplish great things.

Go back to when you were a child and thought you could do anything. What did you want to be when you grew up? What did you want to accomplish? It is not too late to do something significant with your life, I promise. We may have been stripped of our sanity now and again, but we still have so much value, and we have a lot to give.

If you have any doubt about what changing your perspective or view on life can mean to you and your future, go online and watch videos about Nick Vijucic, who was born with no arms and no legs, but impacts the world for good every day.

You may be asking yourself, what do I do next? When you have been told so many times that you are "unemployable" you may start to believe it.

SQUIRREL POINT

Patty was suicidal, depressed, and had racing negative thoughts incessantly. She could not work, and could barely leave the house most days. I helped her grocery shop and helped encourage her. It took her four months to start on the MFM protocols. Then, just a month after starting, she called me, sounding like a different person on the phone: "Now what am I going to do with my life?" she asked. "I feel like I could volunteer or even get a job!" This is a common thought when the brain begins to stabilize and is given a glimpse of normalcy. Unfortunately, she thought she could not afford to stay on the treatment, and slides back into depression when she stops the MFM.

~~~~~~

Most people with mental illness do live and work completely normal jobs and work schedules. However, if you have been on disability, you may wonder what options you could have

134

if you were to fully recover from bipolar. Well, jobs or volunteering your time are always an option, but I like to keep my time my own. Here are some options that can become available to you that may allow you to keep your freedom, and/or disability benefits, while you transition back to work.

Many options offer flexible schedules, and ones that are "self-employed" or 1099 wages offer added benefits through disability and food stamp/child care qualifications in tax breaks for slim profit margins and write offs. This means that if you start a business, but show a loss on your business in the first couple of years you are getting started, the government may still allow you to qualify for benefits.

For example: If you cannot earn more than $700/mo. to retain your disability, but you work a 1099 waged sales job, standard write-offs can be fifty percent, but actual write-offs can be over one hundred percent. This means that you can be making thousands of dollars in "commission income," but after write-offs like business use of cell phone, car, office in home, etc., your tax return could show a negative income at first! I was able to do this for two years while I built up my business.

This allows you to transition out of public assistance only at the time you really can afford to replace your disability income, health insurance, and food expenses. I am not an accountant, or tax or disability benefits attorney, however, so be sure and consult with an attorney about your options. Can't afford an attorney? LegalShield might be a good option so that you can afford one.

SQUIRREL POINT

The legal rights of people with mental illness are not always upheld. If you do not know your rights, it is difficult to enforce them. And how do you get access to your rights when the color of justice is green and you have no green? With a LegalShield membership, for $20/mo. I can call an attorney 24/7 in an emergency situation, like an attempt to be involuntarily hospitalized or protective services inquiring about my children. I have used it for consultations, traffic tickets, to get my will done, and for mental-health-bill of rights related questions. I liked my membership so *much that I started an agency helping others protect and gain access to their rights and have worked that business for seven years!*

http://www.aspenandassociates.com

~~~~~~

"What do I want to be when I grow up, now that I am grown?"
Here are just a few ideas:

- Freelance: writer/blogger/social media expert/web designer/graphic artist
- Trade skill work: plumber, handyman, electrician
- Direct sales/B2B sales/ door-to-door sales
- Consulting/coaching/public speaking
- Business: owner/entrepreneur/real estate agent/loan officer/public notary
- Massage therapist/nutrition/health coach
- Lawn mowing, tree-trimming, pet sitting
- Gardening/raising chickens - selling at farmer's markets
- Art, jewelry-making, crafting, seamstress
- Server/bar tender
- Author/editor, telecommuting, appointment setting
- Home-based businesses/network marketing/MLM

Network Marketing has by far been the best choice for me, but it is *not* for everyone. Traditional businesses were complicated and required too many rules and red tape to comply with for my liking. Network Marketing still has to be treated like a serious job or business and not just a hobby. It has allowed me to go into business for myself with no business training and learn how to make full-time income working only part time hours from home. I do get out and network, talk to people, and attend trainings regularly, however. I have also done B2B sales, freelance writing and editing.

Hope for the best med free life possible, but plan for the worst:
The best-laid plans often do not go as planned, like in the book Of Mice and Men, but being resilient and flexible can help. In your Mental Mindset Recovery™ (MMR) program, I want you to look to the future, not the past. Dream, hope, desire, aspire, but

plan ahead as to not be naive.

Playing "What if I get sick again?"

A good public relations campaign provides provisions for risk management. You should too. Here are the two final pieces of the program that I want you to consider in the process of becoming, being, and remaining Med Free Bipolar. Take note of your symptoms, or lack thereof, and have a plan in place in case they do come back.

Track your symptoms when you have ANY: If you ever feel like you may be relapsing, keep track of when and where you are getting symptoms. Remember that your treatment's efficacy can be thrown off by any number of changes: stomach bugs, prescription medications, diet, sleep patterns, or hormonal changes (guys get them too!). This is normal for everyone, but once you have had bipolar, even a bad day is scrutinized as a relapse.

After I had my tubes tied, my entire hormonal world was turned upside down. I thought I was for sure going crazy again, until I found something called "post tubal ligation syndrome." When I finally found that condition, I had thirty out of forty-five symptoms, and I had been about to go back on medications for moodiness and anxiety! If you feel like your symptoms are returning, first trust your treatments, and then look for hormonal, infections, gut issues or other physical causes for your symptoms.

Have a plan in place, just in case. I have people ask me what in the world I think I am doing? Who am I to tell my story? I am not a doctor, I am not a counselor; how dare I give people "false hope" and "put their lives at risk"? Well, I thought about that for a long time. Aren't our lives already at risk? 25-50 percent of people with bipolar attempt suicide, and 15 percent of people with bipolar succeed. And remember that the drugs meant to save our lives actually decrease our life expectancy by 15 to 25 years![69] If bipolar doesn't overtake us, the medication might. Mania, depression, suicide, or death by increased risky behaviors sounds like a recipe for success doesn't it? I desire to give you the best recipe for success that I can possibly deliver.

This disease can kill people and steal everything, so do not treat it lightly, even when recovery seems complete. It is easy to let your guard down when you have gone years without any traces of mental illness.

That is why I have a safety net, even when I have been healed for so long. Treating bipolar in a new and daring way is like walking out on a tightrope, high above the ground, letting go of the security of the platform in shadows and into the spotlight and fear of the unknown. Hopefully I have made it a lot less scary with the Med Free Method™, but I still recommend a safety net. Walking out on a tightrope without one is just inviting a fall, in my opinion. Having a treatment plan in place is a good idea, there to catch you if you ever fall. I had to use it once since going on the micronutrients, before I had all the resources I do now, and I almost needed it twice.

My one Major Relapse since going Med Free

In 2007, I added the stress of a new career, leaving the home to work for the first time. By this time, I had been off of all medication for five years. I had never replaced my psychiatrist after moving to Idaho, and was living a stigma-free, illness-free, symptom-free existence. I thought I was permanently cured, and let my guard down. In a routine checkup with my primary doctor, she asked me about how I was doing with my two kids, life, and things in general. My health looked superb. I hesitantly told her about my vitamins, and what they were for. She had not known about my psychiatric history, even through the birth of my daughter.

They say patients lie about their medical history: it was at least true for me. She had known me quite a while, and I trusted her as well. She said, "Well, you must have been misdiagnosed. I don't see any way possible that a simple multi-vitamin could attribute to the complete recovery you have shown. There is no reason to keep taking this expensive (about $140/mo. back at the time) multi-vitamin blend. Just switch to an over-the-counter vitamin instead."

I knew based on my childhood and the years leading up to my diagnosis that I had been diagnosed correctly, that it hadn't been just a one-time episode that led to my hospitalization, but I wanted to believe that I no longer needed my micronutrients, and that I had been fully cured. So, when my vitamin supply ran out, we didn't reorder. Within two weeks I was rapid cycling, mixed moods: up, down, and sideways. I was manic, agitated, crying, and scaring my husband to death, as he had never seen me that sick, and not sick at all since our second year of marriage.

I was worse than I had possibly ever been. I probably should have been hospitalized, but we went to the health department for help. They put me on the latest and greatest meds to have hit the market in the last few years while I had been trying that "med-free thing": Lamictal, Abilify, Seroquel. The doctor told me not to look at the side effects when I told her I was sensitive. She said it would help not put "ideas" in my head. I experienced all of them even without looking, and one after another, for three months we tried several different concoctions.

Meanwhile, I reordered my "non-needed" EMPower-plus™ vitamins from Canada, and started taking them again. With the meds not working for me, and the nutrients leveling out my brain once again, I quit taking the meds. I asked the doctor if I could see someone for ongoing monitoring or counseling just in case I ever relapsed. The sliding fee services, she said, were for medication compliant patients only. If I were not fully in the system, I had to be fully out of it. And so I went home and put a plan in place in case I were to ever get sick again.

The Safety Net

Create a Mood Chart to track how you are feeling if you feel symptoms returning.
Create a Safety Net Plan:
See www.medfreebipolar.wordpress.com for an example of what my plan looks like. Include things similar to a "birth plan" for the hospital, but what you would like to see happen if you start to get sick. Include how you feel when you are well and how you feel when you start to have symptoms of bipolar. Talk to your support person about your plan.

Chapter Summary

There is more than just "brain symptoms" to overcome in living a med free life. Years of broken thinking and unrequited dreams take a toll in every aspect of life. Habits can be formed from behaviors caused by illness, and the past can come up to cause unwanted feelings and emotions that are no longer numbed by the misfiring brain or medications.

With Mental Mindset Recovery™, you can learn how to:

- Take action to change your future
- Acknowledge and move beyond the past
- Forgive yourself
- Forgive others
- Feel Gratitude
- Feel Emotions Fully
- Break lingering habits of illness
- Avoid relapses
- Change your words
- Change your thoughts
- Dream again
- Have a plan in place

Action Plan:

- Talk to an empathetic friend or counselor about memories or emotions that may be coming up that have not been dealt with.
- If what you are doing now is not what you want long term, make a gradual change. Suffering is optional.
- Tell yourself five positive affirmations every day in the mirror, and spend time each day envisioning where you want to be in five years

. Write down three things you are grateful for every say.

- Pay attention to your words and thoughts, but be gentle on yourself when you mess up!
- Track symptoms and make a Safety Net Plan.

140

10

How to Turn your Brain Off
Natural Cures for Insomnia

Even though I'm sleeping again, everything still feels a little rickety, like I'm here but not quite here, like I'm just a stand-in for my real self, like someone could just reach over and pinch me and I'd deflate. I thought I was feeling better, but I don't know anymore."

Amy Reed, Author of *Crazy*

Nothing seems to mess up someone with bipolar affective disorder quite as much as irregular sleep. It was disruptions to my sleeping patterns that preluded my first psychotic break, involuntary hospitalization, and bipolar 1 diagnosis.

I think it is important to find sleep aids from natural sources if you have trouble falling asleep on your own. For me, I sometimes need to use several tactics, especially in the fall when I still get some mild hypomanic break-through symptoms.

I understand that sleep is often difficult for the bipolar brain. There are things that can augment and compliment other natural therapies instead of throwing chemicals at a brain that may not tolerate them as well as a brain that is stabilized.

We will look at some of the options that I feel are especially suited to the bipolar brain, and can actually increase the effectiveness of all the other natural treatments for the med free bipolar.

Common Sense Suggestions

- Create a restful environment where you can sleep. My house is always cluttered, but I try to keep all of it out of the bedroom. A clean space can do wonders for the manic or depressed mind. I keep a bottle of lavender water next to my bed to spritz pillows with occasionally. My hubby loves it too. You can also try a lavender essential oil diffuser or a warm lavender bath.

  Make sure you have a good mattress and pillow; the foundations are important. We suffered with a queen mattress that was not very suitable to us, so I sold it on Craigslist to a new college student who loved it, and I was able to buy a king-sized mattress of even better quality for the same price that I had sold my old one. Be creative in solving problems, as it does not always take extra money.

- Have lights on a dimmer switch or use low wattage light bulbs. Low lighting can actually help trigger your body's natural sleep cycle and induce melatonin. Turning on bright lights can interrupt the circadian rhythms.

  Do not watch TV in the bedroom or work on the computer. Do not do stimulating activities such as exercise right before bed. Instead, try journaling, especially in a gratitude journal, listening to classical or soothing music or nature sounds, writing down what is on your mind, or reading a book that is not a page-turner.

- Don't drink alcohol or caffeine as both interfere with sleep patterns. Alcohol may seem to make you sleepy at first, but can disrupt sleep in the middle of the night or increase trips to the bathroom, which is obviously also disruptive.

- Think of things that you are grateful for as you lie in bed. Gratitude can help combat some of the negative self-talk and other things that go along with what may be going on inside your head. Shifting to gratitude is a powerful tool.

- Pray your way to sleep or use imagery to put yourself somewhere relaxing. I like to picture myself as a baby chick, wrapped in the shelter of His wings, and I do not think God minds if I fall asleep talking to Him in the middle of a prayer. Imagining a peaceful setting can be helpful. My dad kept an erratic sleep schedule for thirty years while working as a locomotive engineer for the Union Pacific Rail Road, and he said that imagining the waves lapping at the shore and then receding further and further back into the ocean really helped him fall asleep. I remember him telling me this over a dozen years ago, so it has probably helped me as well.

"He will cover you with his feathers. He will shelter you with his wings. His faithful promises are your armor and protection."
–Psalm 91:4 (NIV)

GOT MILK?

If you drink milk, drinking it at bedtime can help induce sleep, as well as many other health benefits for the brain and gut. Milk is an excellent source of protein and contains nine essential amino acids that are required to meet our physiological needs. We drink raw milk at our house because it is still a live food containing the enzymes and beneficial bacteria (to read more about the safety of raw milk versus pasteurized, whether or not it is easy to buy in your state and where to buy it, go to: www.realmilk.com).

Drinking about 8-16 oz. of milk at bedtime, preferably warm if you like, is not just an old wives tale. My grandmother swears by it, but so does science. Milk contains tryptophan, which the body converts into melatonin, helping you fall asleep very naturally. It has never been quite enough for me to take it alone, but in conjunction with some of my other recommendations, it should help.

HERBAL SLEEP TEAS

Making a cup of tea about an hour before bedtime can

have both relaxation and health benefits. Green tea has been found to be a high anti-oxidant and weight-loss booster, and there are thousands of herbs that are used medicinally around the world that can be as or more effective than prescription medications. Herbs for sleep are no exception, and if you look at the ingredients in most over-the-counter sleep aids, you will find many of them are herb-based. Using these in teas is just another way to get dosing, and can be used in conjunction with most of the other recommendations.

Many herbs can contraindicate with medications however, so be sure to talk with your doctor if you are on other prescription medications. Remember that many drugs are based on herbs, so just because it is natural does not mean that it cannot be powerful.

There are many herbs that can be used in teas to aid in sleep. Valerian is especially helpful in helping people fall asleep, may improve the quality of sleep, and can even help with anxiety. Valerian by itself does not make a very good-tasting tea, so it is best to mask it with something else, like lemon balm and hops. According to Mark Tengler, N.D., in his book, The Natural Physician's Healing Therapies, Valerian should not be taken in conjunction with tranquilizers or antidepressants.

OVER THE COUNTER SLEEP REMEDIES

It took me a long time to find ones that worked for me. Melatonin by itself did nothing, nor did Valerian. It took combining several tactics until I finally found a natural over-the-counter one that worked.

QSleep by QSciences: (see product sources)
I recommend this one the most, but I have to take it with GABA (see below) to shut my busy brain up. The reason I recommend it is my naturopath, Dr. Daniel Nuzum, says the best herbs for bipolar are **valerian, hops, passionflower, and skullcap**. This one has most of them in one absorbable spray form, along with 5HTP. I read an entire book on 5HTP, and it is amazing!
QSleep contains:
• 1mg of melatonin per serving. This specifically propor-

tioned amount of melatonin is gentle enough to not raise melatonin levels in the body higher than are naturally produced when the pineal gland is functioning properly, but sufficient to aid in restful sleep.

- 0.75 mg of 5-HTP per serving. 5-HTP (5-Hydroxytryptophan) is a chemical by-product of the protein building block L-tryptophan. It works in the brain and central nervous system to increase the production of serotonin, which affects sleep. QSleep also contains a proprietary herbal extract to help a person stay asleep throughout the night. The proprietary extract includes the following:

o Cramp bark: The chemicals in cramp bark seem to decrease muscle spasms.

o Feverfew: The feverfew herb has many uses, but it seems to be effective for preventing migraine headaches, which can interfere with sleep

o Ginkgo Biloba: Ginkgo Biloba leaves are generally used to make extracts that improve blood circulation, which might help the brain, eyes, ears, and legs function better.

o Passion flower: The passion flower is a plant often used for insomnia, gastrointestinal (GI) upset related to anxiety or nervousness, generalized anxiety disorder (GAD), and relieving symptoms related to narcotic drug withdrawal. The chemicals in passionflower have been used for calming, sleep inducing, and muscle spasm relieving effects.

o Peppermint: Studies have shown that the leaf and oil from the Peppermint plant provide numerous health benefits. It may aid in helping relieve muscle pain, nerve pain, digestive processes, upset stomach, and inflammation.

o Skullcap: Most commonly, skullcap is used for trouble sleeping, anxiety, stroke, and spasms.

o Valerian root: Valerian is an herb that has been used for centuries to help with anxiety and act as a sleep aid.

According to the Dr. Oz show on April 8, 2014: "Take a supplement that combines Valerian, Hops and Passionflower to help you get a better night's sleep. Dr. Low Dog shared a study that showed *this combination to work as effectively as Ambien*, but without the same side effects." Ambien used to be my sleep drug of choice, and it still amazes me that three little herbs can hold their own in medical research studies to a hypnotic drug that comes with scary side effects like sleepwalking and memory loss.

SLEEP COMBINATIONS CONTAINING GABA:

Sleep aids containing GABA work great for me, and when I looked into why they might work, it made a lot of sense. It does not work for everyone, however, even those with racing thoughts.

GABA- Many natural sleep aids contain GABA (Gamma-amino butyric acid), which is produced by neurons in the brain. It is the primary inhibitory neurotransmitter in our central nervous system. I had finally found my brain's "off switch." GABA can be an excitatory neurotransmitter in a developing brain, so it may have the opposite effect in children and thus is for adult use only.

Theanine- Is an amino acid that comes from green tea and can cross the blood-brain barrier. It is known for its stress relieving properties. It can cross the blood-brain barrier. As an amino acid, Theanine helps you wind down before sleep, and then once asleep, can help you sleep more soundly through the night.

Many sleep blends also contains herbs and melatonin. It may take a little trial and error to find the correct one for your brain.

Homeopathic Calms Forte by HIGHLAND'S

This is a homeopathic sleep remedy that I found at Whole Foods market, but I personally did not find it to work for me. I am including it, however, because mine is not the only bipolar brain out there, and it has worked for some of my other friends.

SQUIRREL POINT

Night terrors, bad dreams, and tossing and turning can be indicative of a B6 deficiency.[70] If the B6 in the recommended product Q96 is not enough to alleviate your bad dreams, add on a little more until you are able to remember pleasant dreams. It is amazing to me that a simple vitamin supplement can literally help people start dreaming again!

~~~~~~

AMINO ACIDS-- An amino acid blend can help with sleep.

5-HTP-- is the precursor to melatonin production, and it worked a lot better for me than melatonin itself.

Reverse Psychology

This may seem too simple, but reverse psychology works even on yourself. Chant over and over: "I am not tired, I am not tired; I can't fall asleep. I must stay awake." There are other visualization tricks beyond counting sheep. You can find more good ideas at: http://www.sleepingtricks.com

Circadian Balancing

In approximately fifty percent of those who suffer from bipolar, the circadian system is unstable. Internal regulation of sleep patterns is weak. Our circadian system is what allows our body to maintain a consistent 24-hour cycle of activity: to sleep at night and be alert during the day at appropriate times. At different times of the day we have increased or decreased activity of certain organs and hormones. These rhythms originate in our brain but are kept in check by external clues such as light and darkness, activities, meals, routines, etc. When these are working, we feel healthy, happy and energized, but when they are out of balance a lot of problems can occur.[71]

Things that can help balance the circadian system include:

- Using an alarm clock that simulates the sunrise.
- Using a light box for 30 minutes in the morning (note: bright light therapy should always be used with dark therapy to prevent switching to hypomania/mania.)
- Dark Therapy- dimming lights 2-3 hours before bed or using low-light glasses can help. Even just a few seconds of bright light can trigger alertness.
- Consistent routines: Eating, drinking, exercising and other daily activities are best done at the same time every day.

Summary Action Plan: APPLICATION

Keeping to a routine and consistent bedtime each night is not just for children, as it can be very helpful in regulating your own circadian rhythms. Create a bedtime ritual that you repeat every night, as this is a powerful signal to your brain to get ready to cease regular activity.

For example: have a small but concentrated cup of tea (Chamomile, valerian, hops, passionflower, skullcap blend would be great!), then dim the lights around the house, play some relaxing music, drink a small glass of milk, brush your teeth, take some GABA, and then read for a while or pray before lights out. Spray the pillow with some lavender water and/or have some calming essential oil blend in a diffuser in your room. I usually need to also wear silicon earplugs and a sleep mask, as even a little light and noise are enough to re-stimulate my senses. It has also been helpful to get my husband a z-quiet device that helps reduce his snoring. If you are the one who snores, be sure to eliminate any underlying causes like sleep apnea. Then spray QSleep under your tongue (I keep it on my bedside table). As your eyes are closed and the room is dark, try some of the visualization tips and tell yourself how you must not fall asleep. Ha ha, I was yawning just writing this!

11

Mind, Body, *Spirit* &
Quantum Psychology

*My delight is in the law of the Lord, and in his law do I meditate day and
night. And I shall be like a tree planted by the rivers of water, that brings
forth his fruit in season, my leaf also shall not wither, and whatever I do
shall prosper."*

Psalm 1:2-3

Spiritual, religious, quantum, and supernatural aspects regarding
mental illness have long been debated. What place does each have
in science, religion or medicine, if any place at all? History is full
of extremes coming from all sides: sorcery-practicing witches who
communed with demons have been burned at the stake, but so
have mentally ill people having a biologically-based psychotic episode who just thought they saw demons.

Psychiatric patients have been subjected to exorcisms, demon casting, while supposedly mentally ill patients have been
healed instantly by the same technique! How can this be? Even the
scientists and skeptics have to admit that there are a lot of things
that science cannot explain that the supernatural and metaphysical and quantum psychiatry can.

How can both sides be completely right or wrong? Could
both sides be right in some instances? Why after so many years

does this debate continue? If someone had a heart attack you would not blame it on a spiritual being stopping his or her heart, or the person willing it so, but the line is blurred when it comes to the mind more than anywhere else.

I believe both neurobiological and/or spiritual reasons exist for some people with mental illness. "According to patient surveys, 77% of individuals who seek medical care feel that their religious or spiritual beliefs are directly related to their health concerns."[72] While fewer than half of scientists believe in God, and less psychiatrists (23%[73]), most medical doctors (76%[74]) believe in God, despite the lack of spirituality incorporated into in Western Medicine practices.

"Strong historical associations between religious beliefs and health stand in stark contrast to the failure of contemporary medicine to address these important issues."[75] The Alternative Medicine arena, however, spares no apologies when it comes to incorporating spiritual or religious practices into their modalities. This is part of why the two schools of medicine, Western and Eastern, appear to butt heads often; but can there be a happy medium? Integrative medicine labels are seeking to only highlight the scientific backings to incorporate modalities such as mindfulness, meditation, and yoga into treatment plans at hospitals and doctor's offices, but there can be spiritual and psychological side effects, as well as ethical and legal dilemmas by doing this.

This raises another problem: if you start including Spiritual/Religious practices into medicine, what happens when your beliefs differ from the practitioner's? Do you want someone else's religious or spiritual beliefs pushed upon you when you go in for a physical or mental condition, or do you just want your beliefs to be respected? What if you went in for a check up and all of sudden they were praying demons out of you? I have had friends who have had that happen! Other legal issues come into play when government-subsidized healthcare is paying for abortions or psychotherapy sessions that include mindfulness, a quasi-spiritual practice that could be construed as blurring the line separating church and state.

The first major separation between "madness" and "demonic possession" came in 1563, and ironically, it was the Quakers and other radically religious people motivated by strong Christian beliefs that pushed for more humane treatment of the "incurably insane."[76]

Today, books like Heaven is for Real, now a major motion picture, and The Spiritual Brain: A Neuroscientist's Case for the Existence of the Soul catch our attention and make us think beyond just what we can see. Maybe after all this time, the more we learn, the less we truly know. Metaphysical/Quantum Psychiatry is an ever-expanding field. The line between science and spirituality, energy work and medicine, which used to be a divide as wide as the Grand Canyon, is trying to make sense of each other and find a place for it all.

> **"We're beginning now to understand things that we know in our hearts are true but we could never measure. As we get better at understanding how little we know about the body, we begin to realize that the next big frontier in medicine is energy medicine. It's not the mechanistic part of the joints moving. It's not the chemistry of our body. It's understanding for the first time how energy influences how we feel."**
> **–Dr. Oz, The Dr. Oz Show**

For me, the consequences of delving into some of these alternative treatments were almost deadly, physically, mentally, and spiritually, while others brought seemingly miraculous healings. I could write a whole book just on this! Several similar detrimental or wonderful experiences have happened to friends of mine, some diagnosed with bipolar and some not.

My purpose in sharing what I know is to help you understand that although most alternative practitioners are well intentioned, great caution needs to be asserted in this area, because it very well could make things worse in the mental health arena, instead of better. Not all things that seem helpful, beneficial, even miraculous are helpful to the bipolar mind.

Informed Consent:

As before mentioned, informed consent is required by doctors, dentists, and practitioners to make sure you are aware of your condition, all treatment options available to you (even alternative/integrative treatments), and pros and cons of each. Unfortunately most practitioners fail miserably in this regard. There are a lot of options out there to wade through. As my version of practicing informed consent, I seek to educate you that there are:

- Medical treatments (i.e.: prescription drugs, surgery, ECT)
- Physical treatments (i.e.: chiropractic, massage, exercise)
- Emotional treatments (i.e.: counseling, EFT/tapping, rapid eye, energy code)
- Nutritional treatments (i.e.: supplements, herbs, diet)
- Religious treatments (i.e.: exorcism, prayer, laying on of hands, fire tunnels, SOZO treatments)
- Spiritual treatments (i.e.: reiki, shamanism, yoga, healing touch, psychic healings)
- Energy treatments (i.e.: acupressure, acupuncture)
- Combination (Spiritual/Nutritional) treatments (i.e.: Chinese medicine, Ayurveda)

The difficult thing is that the lines get crossed and blurred quite often, and each modality may borrow some from another. There may be a physical and spiritual aspect to a treatment that you may not know about or welcome. As a patient, it is your choice what treatments you use or seek, but be sure that you are offered informed consent, and ask pointed questions if you are not sure.

My concern is that practitioners and educators on all sides of the fence: religious, spiritual, medical, even nutritional, do not fully educate about the pros and cons or what their intentions or motives may really be. The doctors may not always disclose side effects and long-term damage caused by medications, and people with spiritual or religious intentions hide behind other modalities. (*For example,* a reiki practitioner [spiritual] who advertises services as just massage [physical] instead of being up front that she also uses reiki in her treatments) I do not agree with the patient becoming victim to other people's agendas, even if the intention is just to help or heal.

A doctor's appointment disguised as a witch hunt would be shut down in a minute, but what about a massage therapist laying on hands with the intent to channel her spirit guide's "healing energy" into you without your knowledge? Some people are ok with this practice, but others are not. It is *your choice* and there should be no judgment or force from any person.

Informed Consent should be practiced among all practitioners as to whether their services are strictly physical, mental, religious or spiritual in nature.

But we as a society cannot be so close-minded as to ignore those who know there is something more than just hallucinations or a chemical balance going on. Committing someone or medicating him/her for seeing an angel, demon, spirit guide, ghost, alien, or animal spirit may prove problematic in the future, especially since it may be part of their beliefs. Perhaps they really did see something. There are several supernatural planes that we do not yet fully understand, if we ever will.

Religion, in turn however, **cannot** continue to deny the reality of legitimate psychosis, delusions, hallucinations and chemical imbalances.

My brother Isaac and I are close, with a lot in common and a lot of differences. He studied Thai massage in Thailand and at an alternative therapy school. He and I have both traveled through Japan and are authors. His book is called *Chewed by Fire: Mowgli's Almanac* (available on Amazon). We could not be more different but are so alike as well. And we both know what we believe. He practices yoga daily, has experienced kundalini awakening, has animal guides, is a really cool falconer, and astral dreams.

I studied Shinto-Buddhism and most of the world religions while living in Japan and acquired an Asian Studies minor in college. I had plans to become a life-career missionary before being disqualified from the missions program due to my mental illness. After that huge disappointment I neglected my belief in God for about ten years and experimented with many paths.

These backgrounds and beliefs make for interesting conversations at holidays, and we both love and respect each other's viewpoints and differing beliefs. We could both be "committed" I am sure for some of our talks: him about spirit guides and me about demons I saw that were disguised as beautiful angel guides. We have both had visions, dreams, and glimpses into the spiritual realms past the veil. We have also both had a psychotic episode that was very different from our spiritual/religious experiences.

But that is what makes our country so great: the freedom to practice out our faith or lack thereof without persecution or ridicule. We should be able to speak our beliefs without fear of a padded room as well.

Be educated on the treatments you get and what they really mean. I do not get to choose or judge your religious, spiritual, or any other beliefs, but I will also not shy away from my own.

I have highlighted some of the Alternative, Quantum, Energetic, Spiritual, and Religious treatments below and some histories so that you may have informed consent before participating, based on your own personal beliefs, whatever they may be.

Based on my personal experience, MOST of the time you CANNOT separate the spiritual side of a practice to just get the physical or medicinal benefits. Even if you don't even believe in a spiritual side at all!

Quantum Psychology -

A very complex and ever-evolving field, the term "quantum psychology" comes from the work of psychologist and philosopher Robert Anton Wilson (RAW). Other related works include Carl Jung, Joseph Campbell, Stanislav Grof, Arnold Mindell, and more. Quantum Psychology, like quantum physics, points to evidence that nothing may be as certain as we think. Quantum psychology looks at more than just the physical or medical explanations of things, such as: what if psychosis, or extreme states, is metaphysical or supernatural in nature or an altered state of consciousness instead of a biological malfunction? Quantum Psychology seeks to explain things like: telepathy, synchronicity, meaningful coincidences, precognitive dreams, and PSI (any unexplained energy transfer or extra sensory perception) or a subjective (phenomenological, existential) experience.

Many "quantum" experiences cannot be explained away by psychosis, as they can often be verified as happening to two people simultaneously, and could perhaps even have been witnessed by a third party.

"Honest Doctor, the hallucinations were real!"

I met the author of the book: Soul Sale: A Rude Awakening, written under the pseudonym Americus Dotter, while in a hot tub at the YMCA. I felt so compelled to speak with her that I started a conversation with the worst conversation starter ever: "Do you come here often?" After we started talking, I found out that she was also a writer, and had even written a book on her psychotic episode where she was diagnosed bipolar. What a coincidence! She also feels her episode was more than just sleep deprivation and post-partum psychosis, although that was legitimately part of it. It was spiritual/religious in nature, and she witnessed things on a spiritual plane that a mere diagnosis cannot explain. It may seem difficult for a doctor or scientist to believe or comprehend, but to those of us who have experienced both psychosis and a spiritual or religious experience, the two are very different!

Praying cannot change psychosis, but can and does stop a demonic attack instantly. Strange, I know, but true. We are more than just physical and mental beings. We are soul, spirit, heart, mind, and body.

"'Love the Lord your God with all your heart and with all your soul and with all your strength and with all your mind'; and, 'Love your neighbor as yourself.'" --Luke 10:27

There are things that not even psychosis can explain away: experiences had by the sane and insane alike. Here is a small excerpt from Dotter's book:

> My psychiatrist told me that the "hallucinations" I was having of "wicked spirits" and "the light" are the same hallucinations that humans have been having since the earliest recorded history. For

years, psychiatry believed that mentally ill people were possessed by the devil, and extreme measures, some very cruel, were adopted to drive out these "demons." Modern medicine has worked very hard to move away from this belief, and I found myself in the awkward position of trying to convince my psychiatrist that this was really what had happened. If humans have had these visions since time began, is it possible that they are not just hallucinations?[77]

I do believe some are just hallucinations, and some are not. It is difficult to argue with people's experiences. Just because we cannot see what someone else is seeing doesn't mean that they are crazy and we aren't.

SQUIRREL POINT

Current Mental Health Books that endorse or introduce spiritual practices as effective treatment:
~Complementary and Alternative Treatments in Mental Health Care:
An entire Chapter on religious beliefs
~Treating Depression and Bipolar Disorder without Drugs:
Recommends reiki, yoga
~The Natural Medicine Guide to Bipolar Disorder:
Discusses Shamanism

~~~~~~

Spiritual Views

The psychiatrist of the future may need to be aware of people's religious and spiritual views before assuming they are just psychotic and committing them for their beliefs. Many people now claim to be "spiritual, but not religious," but those numbers are highest among alternative healers and health practitioners. Before participating in a modality, get to learn a little bit of its history. If you are ok with that practice, then proceed. If you do not want to align with those beliefs, then complete abstinence is the best policy.

"New Age" Spiritual View on Spirit Guides, Astral Advisors, Ascended Masters, and Guardian Angels

"[Spirit guides] are NOT fallen angels. They are simply the equivalent of you – a soul.... Spirit guides come in many different shapes, sizes, forms, and origin. Some come from other galaxies, other dimensions, other planets. They are all souls – energy beings just like our souls. As long as your vibration is high (happiness) and you ask for protection by your Guardian Angel(s) and the god within, heck, your Higher Self even, you really won't encounter any entities that will harm you in any way." –Anonymous

Spiritual view on God: god in all, we too can become gods; the Divine is within us all. We are all connected.

Spiritual Practices

There is a litany of research on how wonderful yoga, meditation, and other modalities are at relieving stress, calming the central nervous system, and boosting brain functioning. I could have just as easily toted all the benefits for an entire book, but I seek to play devil's advocate for part of this chapter and expose some of the dangers these practices could pose for people already susceptible to brain deficiencies. I have personally experienced some of these scarcely known side effects when I practiced yoga and mediation myself. I also have been a recipient of reiki treatments disguised as massage and cranial sacral therapy.

Here, however, I seek to use only sources backed up or provided by yoga, reiki, and meditation experts themselves to provide insight and not my opinion.

Reiki - According to the dictionary, reiki is a healing technique based on the principle that the therapist can channel energy into the patient by means of touch, to activate the natural healing processes of the patient's body and restore physical and emotional well-being." Reiki incorporates the use of "spirit guides" and beings of light to channel this energy through the practitioner into the client. In treating yourself and others: "Reiki psychic surgery can be especially helpful...there are higher sources of help you can call on. Angels, beings of light and Reiki spirit guides as well as your own enlightened self are available to help you. They can help you develop your Reiki practice by directing clients to you and assisting with treatments. They can be of great benefit, but you must have a strong spiritual intention for your work if you are to recruit their aid."[78] The history of reiki comes from Buddhist texts, among others, through Dr. Mikao Usui.

Meditation - Although many start using mediation or mindfulness simply as a way to calm the mind or be present when manic, it can lead to other spiritual experiences. "If you're not aware of meditation dangers, they can unexpectedly come and cause many troubles in your life, such as frightening visions, non-physical contacts, or even **insanity**." –Simona Rich, Experienced Meditator and blogger (emphasis mine). The purpose of mediation is to awaken to the Divine knowledge that you are a god yourself, and that you do not need God. In mediation, "the loss of connection to god must happen for you to realize that you are god....When you meditate you may get many interesting meditation experiences. For example, when I meditate, I sometimes hear conversations in different languages, see certain events from this and other worlds and see different beings." – Simona Rich, Meditator. Rich, as a very experienced meditator, has great articles on the benefits and warnings when it comes to meditation. You can "google" her.

If you are not prepared for this or aware that this may happen, then it can come as quite a shock. If you are, then it can help prevent a psychotic episode. If you are ok with this happening, then meditation may be a viable form of stress release for you.

These modalities are being introduced into psychologist's offices, doctor's offices, and even the schools as benign and medically backed practices, and this is where I take concern. It is not my place to judge these practices, just observe and investigate; I am *for* the recipients having all the facts and being educated enough to decide for themselves what treatments they want to pursue.

Yoga - Yoga means to be "yoked" with Brahman—the Hindu concept of god. The poses are used in idol/deity worship in India, as these "stretches" as we call them, are performed in front of their Hindu deities at the temples. Even the Hindus think it absurd how Americans try to separate the physical exercise from the religious/spiritual aspect of yoga. I studied world religions and Shinto-Buddhism in Japan, visiting temples and witnessing the various Buddhist forms of yoga that can be found in adapted forms across Thailand, China, and other Eastern parts of the world. It is often offending to them that yoga, a sacred spiritual practice of bodily worship, has been secularized for health benefits of movement. If you are not Hindu or Buddhist, then there are other ways to get exercise unless you want the spiritual and physical aspects that go together.

If you want to experience enlightenment and the "kundalini" awakening, then yoga may be a valid option for you. Just know what you are doing before you blindly do it, out of respect to yourself and the practice itself. I used to practice yoga just for the physical benefits that can be achieved, but have abandoned it out of respect to the Hindu/Buddhist religion and because I am not of that faith, nor do I want to worship deities with my body.

This word of caution when it comes to yoga and mental health: although it would seem that yoga is the ultimate relaxation exercise, teaching breathing and centering, many people have had an unexpected side effect: Yogis warn that yoga practice can endanger one's sanity. In describing the awakening of "kundalini" (coiled serpent power) Gopi Krishna records his own experience as follows: "It was variable for many years, painful, obsessive...I have passed through almost all the stages of...mediumistic, psychotic, and other types of mind; for some time I was hovering between sanity and insanity."[79]

One often hears and reads about the dangers of Yoga, particularly of the ill-reputed Kundalini Yoga. The deliberately induced psychotic state, which in certain unstable individuals might easily lead to a real psychosis, is a danger that needs to be taken very seriously indeed. These things really are dangerous and ought not to be meddled with in our typically Western way. It is a meddling with Fate, which strikes at the very roots of human existence and can let loose a flood of sufferings of which no sane person ever dreamed. These sufferings correspond to the hellish torments of the chönyid state…

--C. G. Jung, *The Tibetan book of the Dead*

Carl G. Jung is known as the father of analytical psychology. He was a renowned psychiatrist and spent most of his life studying Eastern and Western philosophies.

"When my kundalini energy awakened I started seeing snakes everywhere: on TV, newspapers, I heard conversations about snakes and even dreamed about them. I felt the kundalini energy moving in me and causing physical discomfort. I felt pressure and buzzing in my ears and during one night it was almost unbearable, I started even fearing that I would not be able to remain sane." –Simona Rich, meditator

Many books talk about these seemingly not-well-known side effects of meditation and yoga. My point is that health care professionals and those of us practicing self-care should be well educated before embarking on practices blindly or recommending them to patients. People already experiencing psychosis or who are susceptible to psychotic episodes should research these topics even more thoroughly before partaking.

Books that discuss this further include: *Kundalini Matters: Science, Psychosis or Serpent* - UK Kundalini Conference 2013, *The Kundalini Experience: Psychosis or Transcendence* by Lee Sannella, *Yoga and the Body of Christ* by Dave Hunt.

Other "Spiritual" modalities:

There are many modalities that are offered to the hurting mental health patient, many of which can be classified as chakra-based healing methods including: reiki, qi-gong, therapeutic touch, healing touch, quantum touch, energetic unwinding, Emo-trance, and craniosacral therapy. More meridian-based energy modalities include: EFT (Emotional Freedom Technique), touch for health, acupressure, Jin Shin Jyutsu®, kinesiology, and, of course, acupuncture.

Other alternative modalities that I feel are more of a spiritual nature, include: shamanic work, matrix energetics, flower essences, angelic healing, dream work, and spiritual inquiry. Muscle testing and water witching may also be along these lines, although widely used and gaining in popularity.

In my search for healing answers, I tried many of these modalities, and although every practitioner thinks that their treatments will help with bipolar, none of them offered real permanent relief in my case on their own, although some provided relaxation and relief from specific symptoms. I have decided to leave expanded definitions out of the Med Free Method™ because they may not be necessary when going through the process of healing. I spent a lot of money and opened myself up to things that almost cost me my sanity.

"Religious" views on neurobiological disorders

Many churches deny the physical, biological, and genetic reality of mental illness (neurobiological disorders (NBD), just as doctors and scientists may deny the existence of a supernatural realm or afterlife. This is damaging to the person who knows their illness is biological in nature, like mine. I find it appalling that most Christian healthcare medi-share programs refuse to help reimburse for psychiatric treatment or hospitalizations. To allow for reimbursement of a heart attack but not a psychiatric break shows how far we as a society have yet to go.

Pastor Steven Waterhouse has written a book with an interesting perspective on this centuries-old debate. It is called: Strength for his People: A Ministry for Families of the Mentally Ill. If you have questions on how to tell whether your issues are biologically based versus spiritually-based, I recommend this book.

Schizophrenia and bipolar can strike anyone, including individuals from deeply religious homes. The concepts of Satan, demons, heaven, and hell are an integral part of many people's beliefs and can be confusing to someone experiencing legitimate psychosis.

The New Testament mentions demons over 100 times including Matthew 8:29, Matthew 10:1, and John 16:11. Even those who have other beliefs or choose to remain skeptical still must relate to Christians and new age spiritual healers and followers who do believe in the supernatural. There is just so much we do not know; neither religion nor science can explain everything.

Many Christians who endure a family member's battle with schizophrenia may have questions about demonic involvement with a loved one and deserve real answers instead of a condescending response which dismisses such concern as nonsense on the part of ignorant people. The Bible itself makes a distinction between disease and possession (Mark 6:13). Thus, Christian theology should recognize the difference also.

My personal experience with "demons" or "dark energetic beings" (or whatever they were):

I promised to be truthful with myself and with you, even if this story completely unravels all my years of research and writing by undermining my credibility with some people. It will sound completely crazy, but happened when I was at my healthiest mentally. Since sharing, dozens of others have shared with me similar experiences, so I know I am not the only one.

At the time of this story, however, even I thought I was slipping back into the darkest insanity I had yet experienced.

I have mentioned my "bipolar relapse" in 2007 when I quit my micronutrient protocol because my doctor said I must have been misdiagnosed and I could just take any multi-vitamin instead. But in October of 2011, I thought I was getting sick yet again. However, this time it was **spiritual in nature** and *not* mental illness.

In the months leading up to October, I had been feeling

well and completely whole mentally. I had decided to more aggressively do research for my book: a version I thought would look different than the one I am writing. It was going to contain information on all the alternative modalities that are available today. I was going to try them all. It was also going to be written anonymously.

But instead of finding improvements to my mental health with each treatment I started...I started presenting psych symptoms for the first time in five years! My mental health started to decline, but in a newly strange and terrifying way. All the "textbook" symptoms were there, but in a way that was not familiar to me in how they had presented before I ever got well. I even started tracking symptoms again, something I had not needed to do in years. I sought help and considered going back on meds, seeing a counselor and clinic with med-management as backup for the first time in five years. I had spread out my safety net, even though I did not feel like I needed medication, yet.

I felt like a failure on my med-free journey. I would never be able to write to help people now. I felt like a fraud. I was getting sick, despite my well-developed methods.

Then, weird things started happening. My husband was having dreams of demons and my children all started having night terrors at once. One life-changing night, it was like a massive swirl of darkness filled me. Rage, mixed moods, rapid cycling, and visions of death filled me. It was unlike anything I had experienced before, it was so much worse, and I wanted to throw myself out the window to stop the torture. I had never felt such extreme states before.

I went upstairs to be alone lest I hurt someone or something. The emotional and physical pain escalated and crescendoed. I stared in the mirror but the eyes were not blue like mine, they were black and unfamiliar. I was scared. I grasped at every "remedy" I knew. I swallowed choline and inositol, sprayed lavender and tried to do the yoga poses on the floor I had learned at the YMCA before I had studied the spiritual chord connected to yoga.

I wanted something, anything to relieve the torture going

on in my head and body. I hit the button on the radio but heard no music coming from it, only the screams in my head followed by deafening silence. It felt like my ears were stopped up, like something was stabbing at my eardrums from the inside. Then something dark swam and swirled before my eyes and the room went black. I could not see, and I thought I had gone blind instantly. Falling to my knees I leaned forward into child's pose.

I held my hands upright in front of my face but nothing but blackness was seen through my open eyes. I was blind and deaf! Bipolar had never **felt** like this before, even in my complete psychosis. Finally: exhausted, spent, desperate, and I don't know why, as I had not prayed in a very long time, I screamed:

"God, Jesus, Jesus, Help Me, help me PLEASE!" I do not know if I even meant it, least of all expected it to work!

Instantly, the blackness dissipated just like it had come on: black swirls exited my eyes and I watched as they dissipated into the ceiling! And all the pain and symptoms disappeared instantly. The swirls of rage, anger, hatred, physical suffering, and mixed episodes were gone! My eyes were working, seeing and my ears unstopped. Immediately I heard a song fill the room, clear and actually quite loud, the volume turned up high in my desperate attempt to hear the radio when I had turned it on. It was a song I had never heard before. I felt like the words were directed into me, filling me, as if the artist had written them just for this moment, just for me.

"Be still, there is a Healer
His love is deeper than the sea
His Mercy is unfailing
His arms, a fortress for the weak"

As the music played, I (or my spirit?) was transported out of my bedroom into a vision so real it felt like I could touch it, enveloping me 360 degrees. I was floating above a desert, panning in as if from a plane or as if I were flying. I saw a black tree in the distance, more like a dead stick standing up out of the cracked spent land scorched along a dry riverbank. The roots were shriveled and gnarly, spilling over the bank before they died in desperate reach of water.

As I got closer to the tree I could feel its pain, knowing that it had once been beautiful but was now lost. I could relate to how it felt. However, the closer I got the more detail began to emerge. The roots started moving and the black trunk turned to birch white. Leaves started to appear on the branches and life began to stir into the ground and air. At that moment a flash flood of water raced through the riverbed, washing over the roots and covering them with Living Water. The thirsty tree drank, and I could feel its joy at coming back to life.

I was standing at the foot of the tree now and was looking up. The once hot dry ground was spring lush, and the grass between my toes was the softest velvet. Colors existed that I had never seen before and enveloped me in warmth.

But I was bitter even standing there, hurt from my past religious upbringing and mental torments. Many times in the past when I had cried out to God for help I had been met by nothing. How could a God who supposedly loves us cause such pain? I remember sarcastically thinking, "What?! Is this stupid tree supposed to turn into a cross?" It did not disappoint, with two branches outstretched from the trunk in cross-like fashion; but then the rest of the details of the tree filled in as it came back to life. A black and white familiar trunk came into detail. At the same moment I gasped, realizing it was an **aspen** tree, I heard a Voice, clear and sweet and familiar from years ago, when He told me to hang on, say: "I died JUST for You, Aspen!"

In that instant I was back in my room, still on my knees in child's pose, but I could faintly hear the last echoes of that Voice, reverberating through the land and the distant canyons, going out to all who are lost, seeking them out and just asking them to believe and call upon His name when they have died inside: Jesus. Tears streamed down my face, and the song picked up right where it had left off, although it seemed I had been gone a long time in that desert oasis.

"Be still, there is a river,
That flows from Calvary's tree
A fountain for the thirsty
Your Grace, that washes over me
Let Faith arise
Open my eyes
Let Faith arise
You are faithful God, forever"
--Chris Tomlin- "I Lift My Hands"

It was the most real experience of my entire life, and the years have not diminished the memory in the slightest. I will be careful about opening myself up like that again to spiritual things I thought did not exist. The dark energies, or whatever they were, that had "possessed" me almost drove me to throw myself out of a window to make them stop tormenting me. I related to the swine in the Bible that drowned themselves to be rid of the demons inside them.

I cannot fully explain how I know that what I experienced during that period was all spiritual warfare in nature and not mental illness, but I do.

After that night, we prayed over the house and our children. Their night terrors stopped even though they did not know what had happened. Apparently *their* nightmares were not caused by a B6 deficiency. When you are a mom and you see your child having nightmares every night for months and then they go away all of a sudden, you know. You just know. A few days later the spirit veil lifted for three hours, and that is when I saw demons disguised as angels; but that story is best saved for a book of "fiction" it is so unbelievable, even to me. I can imagine you as the reader throwing my book across the room right now if you have never had an experience like that! I would not have believed me either before it happened.

Like I said, having experienced both delusions and psychosis, and something else of a spiritual nature, they were very different from each other, but close enough to be confusing. If you have had similar spiritual happenings, I would love to hear your experiences.

All of my other "bipolar symptoms" left that night as well and have not returned since! The rapid-cycling, mixed moods, irritability, rage, confusion, paranoia, anxiety, self-doubt, nightmares, mania, depression, suicidal thoughts, and desire to self-harm that I had started tracking just the previous weeks subsided in an instance, with a prayer. I can't explain it. Prayer had never worked before when I was "biologically" suffering from an episode. But I know this was not all in my head. It was not a delusion. Now, even years later, I can close my eyes and still feel the velvet grass between my toes.

The book cover is symbolic of many things: the brain, the digestive and central nervous system, the dark/light, sick/well, happy/sad juxtapositions of bipolar, but mainly this unforgettable vision that changed my life and my future.

It is a reminder that my complete healing is not all of my own doing, but I am thankful that the steps that healed me are duplicable, both the physical and spiritual steps. I share this, despite the fact that it could undermine my work, so that you can have as many tools in your toolbox as possible against a disorder that thousands of years and thousands of experts have not been able to fully understand. I don't pretend to either.

Could it be that some delusions are rooted in the unbalanced brain, while others are rooted in the spiritual and supernatural realms? I know this one instance would be the exception and not the rule, as all my other symptoms over the years were not alleviated in any way through prayer, and I would never undermine what each person goes through, but this episode I just can't explain any other way than supernaturally miraculous. There are just some things we don't know and can't explain. Just because you have not experienced something similar doesn't mean that it does not exist. You have probably experienced things that no one else could ever comprehend.

Chapter Summary

Mind, Body, Heart, Soul, and Spirit are all inter-connected and should not be treated as sole and separate. Science, religion, and medicine collide on many levels, but the treatments of the future will not be able to make such clear distinctions, as it becomes more and more apparent that we are spiritual and energetic beings as well as physical and mental.

Supernatural occurrences that science cannot explain can and do happen regularly, to the sane and mentally ill alike. My experience and Americus Dotter's could have been a psychotic delusion, but having experienced true psychosis and something of a spiritual nature, they were very different experiences. Practitioners who treat people with or without a diagnosis should not assume that everyone who talks about a "spiritual" experience is delusional, psychotic, or diagnosable. They need to ask: "What IF?" What if my client really did see an angel and isn't crazy? What IF my client is not hallucinating and is telling the truth?

However, practitioners or people who treat coming from a religious or spiritual nature should be up front about their intentions, agendas, history and potential side effects of their methods. They should not cast out demons or channel spirit guide energy without full-disclosure and permission.

Just as doctors and dentists are held to practice informed consent, alternative practitioners should be as well.

If you are ok with treating your condition with prescription drugs, or Reiki, or Yoga, or Prayer, then do, and don't ever let anyone make you feel bad for doing whatever you feel is best for you. God gave you free will and choice for a reason.

No one should be able to make decisions for you regarding your body, mind, and spirit. Your religious and spiritual beliefs are yours and yours alone and should be respected without judgment. When you make informed decisions about the treatments you get and consider, look into the history, the outcomes, and the warnings or possible spiritual side effects. The ultimate goal is to be well, whole, and of a sound mind with a hope and a future.

12

Resolving Rage, Racing Thoughts, Sound Sensitivity, & Physical Problems

My creative energies soar; I feel like I can do anything. This high can last for days, weeks, or even months. Eating and sleeping are just an afterthought. Then all at once, a million thoughts come rushing in. I can't keep up

Janine Crowley Haynes, Author of My Kind of Crazy

Some of the side effects that accompany bipolar are atrocious. No one who has not experienced it can possibly understand how for some, noises feel like they are stabbing you in every cell, how the rage can overtake you and cause pain, and the racing thoughts can make your head feel like it will explode if it won't turn off.

I am grateful that I have found fast natural cures to alleviate the symptoms of bipolar.

People keep saying that most mental illness is a "chemical imbalance," but will not say a chemical imbalance of what and what causes the chemical imbalances? What they mean by this is an imbalance of the "chemical messengers" called neurotransmitters. It does make sense to me that these are imbalances of our natural hormones, neurotransmitters, and nutritional deficiencies. However, it is important to know that most of the education regarding chemical imbalances has been perpetuated by pharmaceutical companies and not backed by science according to experts like Dr. Kelly Brogan among others.

The neurotransmitter's job is to transport messages from one brain cell to the other. Neurotransmitters affect attention, memory, personality, and even physical health. When these are imbalanced or not being utilized by the body correctly, then it is no wonder there is a "chemical imbalance." The amazing thing about natural supplements is that your body recognizes them as being usable, and if it does not need them, will flush them out or even store them for later use.

It has been important for me to know what I am feeling and what might be beneficial at that point in time in order to self-select a natural remedy applicable to my symptom.

This can be more complicated than it sounds at times. Do I need an "upper," or a "downer"? Some of the supplements mentioned here are powerful, and may not be recommended for people who tend to swing really high or really low, as some of them could trigger mania or depression; you need to decide for yourself if it is possible to take something that could hurl you into depression or mania.

Each of us is unique, even with the same diagnosis, and what has worked well for me may not work the same for you. I feel, however, that if you are reading this book you should be properly educated and given options. Our bodies and minds have an amazing ability to heal when given the necessary ingredients, and can heal even after years of episodes and damage from medications. The main reason we do not heal is that we feed our brains chips and chemicals and expect it to make an organic salad out of the ingredients.

It was helpful to me in my self-healing to learn which neurotransmitters were "On Switches" and which ones were "Off Switches," like I alluded to in the chapter regarding sleep. I was watching my husband fall asleep one night and was amazed at the whole thirty seconds it seemed to take him to go to sleep. The next night I asked him:

"How do you do that?"

"Do What?" He asked.

"Fall asleep like that, so fast, so easily?" I said. He thought about it for a second and then said,

"I don't know, I can just turn my brain off for the day and go to sleep, it's kind of like a switch. I decide I am going to sleep, and I do."

"Well," I replied, "either my switch is broken, or I did not come with one." I felt totally short-changed! It seems I have never been able to consistently turn my brain off like that, but I have finally gotten the sleep thing under control (see insomnia chapter), and am thankful to have found things that work for tough situations.

But how do these supplements work? Our bodies need the proper balance of these neurotransmitters, and when they are imbalanced, it only makes sense that symptoms will appear. It is a good idea to keep a mood chart and know yourself well. I charted for a while when I first started treating my bipolar naturally, but only chart now if I feel like I am going through a difficult-enough time to warrant watching myself more closely, which has been exactly twice in eleven years.

- **Dopamine- Frontal Lobe- Voltage- "ON" switch**
- **Acetylcholine-Parital Lobe- Regulates Speed- "ON" switch**
- **GABA- Temporal Lobe- Rhythm- "OFF" Switch**
- **Serotonin- Occipital Lobe- Harmony- "OFF" Switch**

Dopamine- Voltage- "ON" switch

Dopamine —controls pleasure/reward centers, movement, memory, and emotions. It is a little complicated because it can be an excitatory and inhibitory neurotransmitter, according to Integrative Psychiatry. Dopamine is the precursor to norepinephrine and epinephrine.

Symptoms of Dopamine imbalance:

Too much dopamine can cause:

- Mania
- Euphoria
- Schizophrenic tendencies like hallucinations and para-noia
- Elevated testosterone
- Increased sex drive
- Pleasure seeking
- Anger/Agitation/Rage
- Anxiety
- Alertness/Restlessness
- Racing thoughts
- Lack of emotions/feeling

Too little can cause:

- Depression
- Fatigue
- Procrastination
- Low libido
- Addictive behaviors
- A need for caffeine and other self-medicating substances
- Weight gain and more.
- Excessive emotions

Clumsiness (Dyspraxia) can also be attributed to low and high dopamine levels!

What causes Dopamine imbalances?

It is theorized that chronic stress, increased cortisol levels, insomnia, certain prescriptions including anti-depressants, drug use, vitamin deficiencies, sugar and refined foods, processed foods, food dyes, thyroid problems, digestive issues, leaky gut, and even Parkinson's disease are just some of the reasons that someone might develop imbalanced dopamine levels.

What helps balance Dopamine?

Dopamine is synthesized from the amino acid Tyrosine (See Below). Supplementation with a well-balanced micronutrient supplement like Q96 that includes vitamins, minerals, amino acids, and anti-oxidants can help, but you can also increase dopamine through foods.

Dopamine increasing foods that contain tyrosine include: raw almonds (especially soaked and sprouted), ripe avocados, ripe bananas, dairy products (especially raw, fermented, or probiotic-rich like kefir), lima beans, pumpkin seeds, and sesame seeds. (See more in chapter on diet) There are other all-natural dopamine-increasing supplements on the market as well.

Acetylcholine –Regulates Speed- "ON" switch

Acetylcholine was the first neurotransmitter to be identified in the early 1900s. It is a derivative of choline and acetic acid (acetyl) and is important to the peripheral nervous system (PNS) and central nervous system (CNS). Acetylcholine is involved in learning, memory, speed, and reaction time. It also stimulates muscle tissue as a growth hormone. It is considered to be involved in Alzheimer's disease.[80]

Symptoms of Acetylcholine imbalance:
Too little:
- Difficulty remembering names and/or faces, birthdays, anniversaries
- Trouble remembering lists, directions, instructions, and common facts like times tables. (This was a chronic problem for me growing up, I could never memorize my times tables despite having straight A's in every subject. Math was a nightmare!) Some struggle with spoken or written language.
- Forgetting where you put things (e.g. keys)
- Making simple mistakes at work
- Confused or slowed thinking, difficulty forming sentences
- Disorientation
- Social withdrawal, ambivalent feelings toward life or lacking in passion and purpose
- Feeling despair or lack of hope and joy.
- Loss of creativity and imagination, motivation

Too much:
- Paranoia
- Brain racing
- Flight of idea
- High creativity
- Attention Deficit

What causes low Acetylcholine?
One or more of the following can cause acetylcholine deficiency:
- Choline deficiencies (choline is like a vitamin, it's very important to the brain and found in beef liver and whole eggs, but especially the yolks, so always eat the yolks!)
- Inadequate supply of vitamin B1 & B5
- Chronic stress, fatigue, inadequate sleep
- Elevated blood sugar levels and insulin resistance
- Environmental toxins such as mercury (like from amalgam tooth fillings), lead, aluminum, PCB's (like what is found in most plastic containers), fertilizers, pesticides, and EMF exposure (computers, cell phones, and other devices)
- Over-methylation

What helps balance Acetylcholine?
Supplements such as choline bitartrate* and CDP-choline raise levels of acetylcholine; phosphatidyl choline (also called lecithin), serves as sources for acetylcholine synthesis. Ginseng and ginkgo Biloba* are herbal alternatives. Reducing toxins in the environment and using natural products in the home and especially on your skin can help reduce the toll on your body's ability to self-detox. *Choline bitartrate and gingko Biloba are in my daily-recommended product: Q96.

GABA- Temporal Lobe- Rhythm- "OFF" Switch

"GABA is a brain chemical that inhibits impulses between brain cells."[81] Gamma-amino butyric acid (GABA) controls the brain's rhythm. People with GABA dominant brains are usually stable, logical, reasonable, and grounded.

Too little:
- Mind instability
- Racing thoughts
- Feel jumpy/on edge
- Anxiety
- Severe Physical Pain
- Heart Arrhythmias
- Drug and Alcohol Abuse
- Sweaty, clammy hands
- Low stress tolerance

Too much:
- "Caregiver syndrome"- help others w/o regard to self
- Lightheaded
- Sleepy
- Slow heart beat

What causes GABA deficiencies?
- Glutamine deficiency (a precursor to the production of GABA)
- B1, B6, zinc, manganese, and iron deficiency
- Inadequate sleep
- Progesterone deficiency
- Mercury and lead exposure
- Alcohol withdrawal
- Excessive alcohol
- Chronic stress events such as death in the family, divorce, moving, job loss, PTSD

GABA can be taken in supplement form.
Foods that help balance GABA- Sprouted Almonds, banana, broccoli, brown rice, halibut, lentils, oats, potato, walnuts, and whole wheat grains, properly prepared
(L-Glutamine, the precursor for GABA, as well as the B vitamins and minerals are in Q96)

Serotonin- Occipital Lobe- Harmony- "OFF"

Switch

"We now know that nutrients can play a strong role in influencing mood. For example, the essential amino acid tryptophan, found in protein-rich foods such as eggs, meats, and milk, is used by the body to make serotonin, a neurotransmitter that regulates emotional tone and soundness of sleep."[82]

Too much: Serotonin Syndrome:[83]
- Confusion, agitation or restlessness
- Dilated pupils, headache
- Changes in blood pressure and/or temperature
- Nausea and/or vomiting, diarrhea
- Rapid heart rate
- Loss of muscle coordination or twitching muscles
- Shivering and goose bumps, heavy sweating

Too little:
- Strong sugar cravings
- Indifference to situations you typically would care deeply about
- Excessive worrying
- Inability to fall and stay asleep
- Moderate to overwhelming sadness
- Feeling worse and agitated during bad/dark weather
- Anxiety during low stress situations
- Impatience without explanation
- Fatigue when you should feel rested and energized
- Cognitive impairment (inability to focus, poor memory, lack of mental clarity)
- Negative thoughts with no apparent cause, agitation
- Mania/obsession, mood swings

Serotonin enhancing foods:
Avocado, chicken, cottage cheese, duck, granola, oat flakes, turkey, wheat germ, wild game, yoghurt.

So for me, sometimes it has felt like I have two "ON" switches and no "OFF" switches. This makes sense to me because when I was hypomanic or manic, I was all go and no stop. I did not think about consequences, ramifications, other people's feelings, or even think about the need for sleep. But when I was depressed, it was the opposite. Once my "on" neurotransmitters had been depleted, the other ones seemed to take over.

Natural Medicines for Psychiatric Disorders and Specific Symptoms

None of these supplements individually would have allowed me to remain prescription drug-free without the EMPowerplus™ Q96 as my foundation, but I feel at times that the Q96 does not curb all break-through symptoms, and that I occasionally need to take one or more of the following during stressful or difficult times.

If you do not notice any benefits in just two weeks, stick with each thing for at least three months, as nutrition and supplements can work more slowly than prescriptions. Then look back, and if you are not happy with your health and symptom management, try an additional tip.

I have listed these by categories of symptoms. I equate this to using over-the-counter medicines, like taking cold medicine for a cold, or aspirin for a headache. I may take one thing for "surround sound" and anxiety, and something different for racing thoughts if they occur.

For foundational Daily Mood Stabilization AND general health:

EMPowerplus™ Q96-- The most independently researched micronutrient blend in the world. Includes a bio-available blend of thirty-six vitamins, minerals, amino acids, and antioxidants.
Where to buy: see product resources page.

Lithium Orotate (120mg) (see Chapter Three for more complete info)
Where to buy: most health food stores or online.

Lithium Orotate is a safe, over-the-counter mineral supplement that can be safely used in place of Lithium Carbonate.

Cell Salts: Young Living's AlkaLime; Hyland's Biplasma Tablets

Homeopathic Remedies for Bipolar:
- Bryonia
- Chamomilla
- Natrum Muriaticum Pasiflora
- Sepia

Herbal remedies:
- Chamomile flowers
- Hops flowers
- Passion Flower
- St. John's wort herb (Bipolar type II, not type I)
- Skullcap herb
- Valerian root

DHEA- DHEA is a natural hormone, made by the adrenal glands that has been studied quite extensively and has shown to: improve mood and energy, boost sex drive (in women more than men), help fight disease, and even influence longevity.[84] In a three-month study, middle-aged volunteers who were given 50 mg of DHEA nightly for three months reported enhanced energy, deeper sleep, improved mood, more relaxed feelings, and an improved ability to handle stress.[85] Other studies have purported DHEA could also be beneficial in treating cancer, diabetes, heart disease, lupus, and obesity. Some call it "the fountain of youth," as DHEA levels naturally decline as we age, and supplementing could, hypothetically, increase lifespan.

Possible Side-effects: Increased libido, longer lifespan, better mood, better sleep, better moods

Where to Buy and What Kind? DHEA can be purchased from your local health food store, but a few things should be considered on types. Do not buy the "natural" form often called the precursor to DHEA: natural yam extract, it must actually be processed into DHEA, according to Seymour Lieberman, PhD, who is considered the foremost expert in the field with 55 years experience! Watch out for labels like "natural DHEA" and "DHEA precursor complexes." DHEA levels can be checked by a physician to find out if you are low, however, many doctors recommend supplementation for people forty and up. Dosing recommendations vary widely: from 5 mg per day up to 100 mg per day for anti-aging outcomes. Talk to a physician familiar with DHEA or start small and titrate up if there are no noticeable benefits.

Mania:

Herbs: Kava Kava- According to WebMD, this root from the South Pacific can be used (with caution due to some reports of liver damage on high doses) to treat:

- Anxiety, stress
- Restlessness and sleep problems
- ADHD
- Epilepsy, psychosis, depression, headaches

There has also been some success treating Uterine Tract Infections (UTI).

Homeopathic Remedies for agitation and mania:
1. MoodCalm™ by NativeRemedies
www.nativeremedies.com

Rage:
1. Extra Q96 (2-6 capsules extra to total 6-10/day)
2. Inositol
3. Calcium and Magnesium
4. Homeopathic remedies for rage can number close to one hundred; seeing a qualified naturopath is a good idea when it comes to homeopathy.
5. Lithium Orotate

Anxiety/Agitation/Stress:
1. Holy Basil Trinity Blend

2.   Inositol- (A B-vitamin complex, inositol works on a cellular level to quickly calm anxiety, paranoia, and hyper-sensitivity. I prefer the powder form over the capsule, because it has almost no taste to it and works sometimes in as little as three minutes)

Calm:

1.   Q96
2.   DHEA
3.   5-HTP
4.   Calcium and Magnesium

"Surround Sound," Sensory issues i.e.: Extreme Sensitivity and Sensory Processing Disorder:

1.   Inositol (Do not underestimate this remedy!)
2.   Q96

Depression:

1.   5-HTP
2.   SAM-E
3.   St. John's Wort
4.   DHEA

Racing Thoughts:

1.   Phosphatidyl Choline -- Claims to support healthy liver function, but has been used for quieting racing thoughts.
2.   Inositol
3.   Q96
2.4.   Lithium Orotate

Dyspraxia (Clumsiness)

1.   EMPowerplus™ Q96
2.   Choline
3.   Egg Yolks
4.   DHA
5.   Fish Oil/Omegas

6. Thyme
7. Vitamin E

Yeast/Candida:

Article: (www.mindbodygreen.com)
10 signs you have it and what to do about it article

1. Caprylic Acid/Boric Acid
2. High-potency Probiotics (30+ Billion)
3. Olive Leaf Extract
4. Oregano Oil
5. Yoghurt
6. Cranberry Juice
7. Basil Tea
8. Garlic
9. No douching

Urinary Tract Infections:

1. D-Mannose- Works by flushing out bacteria. Take at first sign of pain! I have used this several times and it works amazingly well!
2. Cranberry supplements
3. Kava Kava
4. For pain: Yazo makes an OTC tablet almost identical to the ones the doctor gives that numb the pain and turn your urine bright orange

General Infections

Article: (www.greenmedinfo.com)
36 Natural Alternatives for Infections

Bleeding Gums/Periodontal Issues:

1. Oil Pulling (with coconut oil or sesame oil)
2. Blue Light Therapy
3. OralMD, Herbal Mouthwashes and Toothpaste
4. Calcium and Magnesium Supplements
5. EMPowerplus™ Q96

6. Whole food supplements
7. CoQ10
8. Vitamin D
9. Fermented Cod Liver Oil
10. Hydrogen Peroxide

I highly recommend the book: Cure Tooth Decay Naturally

Digestive Issues/Leaky Gut:

Article: (www.mindbodygreen.com)
8 Supplements to Heal a Leaky Gut

1. Med Free Method™ steps 1-3
2. Probiotics
3. L-Glutamine (in Empower™ Q96)
4. Digestive Enzymes
5. Hydrochloric Acid
6. Slippery Elm

If still not having improvements, see Full "GAPS" diet at: www.gaps.me

Food Allergies

1. Elimination Diet
2. Gluten-free Diet
3. The Meyers Way™

Brain Allergies

1. Article on Brain Allergies:
http://www.alternativementalhealth.com/articles/brainalle rgies.htm
2. Book: Brain Allergies, Wheat Belly, Grain Brain

Digestive/Elimination Issues:

1. Probiotics
2. See Full GAPS Diet at: www.gaps.me
3. Increase HCL and Enzymes (See Step One in Book)
4. 1 tbsp. Olive Oil per day
5. Coconut Oil as much as can eat/day and in Coffee

6.   Baking Soda/Epsom Salts in Bath
7.   Celtic Sea Salt Bath
8.   Enema
9.   Magnesium Oil
10.   Digestive Enzymes

Detox: The Misner Plan (**http://www.misnerplan.com**)

Betain Hydrochloric Acid (HCL)—Many people produce less HCL as they age, but many people with bipolar seem to produce less from the beginning. One of my most basic theories of what caused me to eventually develop bipolar traits is that I simply did not produce enough HCL to help digest and glean nutrients from my food from the very beginning of life. If you have digestive issues, lacking HCL could be the cause.

HCL Activator — An "activator" for HCL helps it work more effectively. The one I use is by Premiere Research Labs and is a combination of: tomato concentrate, turmeric, royal jelly (queen bee food), pine bark extract, natto concentrate (fermented non-GMO soy), coriander leaf, oregano leaf. Thank-fully it comes in a capsule so I do not have to taste it. If you have ever had natto, it is a delicacy in Japan, and it stinks. I did not like it, but as for fermented foods, it is very, very good for you.

See Step One in Med Free Bipolar for foods that increase digestive enzymes.

Heart Problems/Cholesterol issues

1.   Book: *Put your Heart in your Mouth* by Campbell-McBride & *No More Heart Disease* by Ignarro
2.   CoQ10
3.   L-Arginine
4.   L-Cysteine

Libido: Too high or too low sex drive

Adaptogenic herbs can increase or decrease sex drive depending on the individual. They make a huge impact on the decreased libido side effects that come with many psychotropic medications, especially anti-depressants.

1. Guarna
2. Black cohosh
3. Damiana
4. Idaho Blue Spruce essential oils and other blends

Many other things can be natural aphrodisiacs: anise seed, cardamom seed, cayenne pepper, cinnamon bark, cloves, coriander, cumin seed, curry, fennel, garlic, ginger, mustard seed, nutmeg, parsley, rosemary, sage, turmeric, and vanilla.

QSciences, a company based in UT, has a great "Qssentials" pack that includes all of the herbs necessary for libido (herbs), mental and physical well being (Q96), heart (CoQ10), gut (probiotics). They have an energy pack or caffeine free option.

Bed Wetting and Night Terrors:

1. EMPowerplus™ Q96- Bed-wetting is a sign of toxicity overload. Minerals help chelate the toxins out of the body, thus reducing the bladder's urge to get rid of them spontaneously in the middle of the night. This will be discussed more in book three of the Med Free Method™ Book Series: Med Free Child.

2. Vitamin B6- Night Terrors are indicative of usually one of three things: a vitamin B6 deficiency, toxicity, or spiritual/home-life issues. Watching horror movies, violent video games or even having them present in the home can also trigger night terrors. I suffered from night terrors as long as I can remember. When I found out about B6 and it's link to night terrors and pleasant dreams, it took me six months of additional supplementation before I started to have "pleasant dream recall".

CONCLUSION

The true meaning of life is to plant trees, under whose shade you do not expect to sit.

Nelson Henderson

Spring is settling in along the creek in my back yard. My husband listened to parts of the book tonight he had never read. We both tear up at the years of pain, while tears of gratitude comingle for what our life looks like now. It is so difficult to revisit a time that seems as remote as the moon. Life has been mostly good these past ten years, exceptional to what it could have been. That doctor who told me I should not have children can go eat crow. I hear my miracles laughing: 12, 8 and 5 years old now. They are healthy. They are whole and so am I. I made it through one pregnancy 'un-medicated' and two more 'med free' and free of the need for meds. Med Free. Diss-order Free. Symptom Free.

I am grateful I was born now, instead of when I might have been burned at a stake or chained to an asylum's walls, lobotomized or convulsively shocked. I am hopeful for a time when mental health patients are actually treated as medical patients and not criminals, escorted to hospitals in ambulances instead of cop cars in handcuffs or locked behind bars. But I am very grateful for the advance of doctors, for the medication that got me out of psychosis. I am eager for the future of mental health care and the changes we will see when others join this grassroots movement for natural healing. I believe we are on the cusp of a paradigm shift.

My mind wanders as the chickens are being chickens — scratching behind me along the bank. I appreciate their company and they soothe me in a way I never imagined possible. I carried a glass of Riesling out near the coop and the creek and plopped a chair down, soothed by their frantic search of whatever it is they find just beneath the surface of the soil. White wine goes great with chicken in more ways than one. There is health here. There is peace here. I am mindful of the breeze, the pecking order of life, and the sun moving down in steady progress.

A smile creeps upon my face as I remember one more vision: It is 2009. I sit in a women's conference writing down my goals. We are gluing magazine pictures down on a vision board. I have all the prerequisites stuck down: travel, a car, happy family and a maid, most importantly. I am proud of what I have accomplished thus far compared to where I had been: I am in the top 500 out of 100K sales reps and it is the height of my career, but my goals are set on higher achievements and I stretch my wings and strut at the thought of where I would like to be in five more years. I am optimistic about the future in a way I had never before thought possible when I was sick and on public assistance. I look at my dream board. Something is missing. I lean back in the chair and close my eyes.

"Ok, Lord. Where do YOU see my life in five years?" I ask.

Be careful what you ask for. A vision more clear than magazine clippings downloads instantly. I am standing on a stage in front of a large audience. I am speaking but I cannot hear what I am saying. I pan in closer and realize that I am talking about bipolar. "That would never happen," I mock the vision. "That doesn't even make sense. If I were to ever speak on stage, it sure wouldn't be about bipolar!"

I hear that familiar Voice say: "Get Ready."

The vision and paralyzing fear is so real I start to tremble and run to the bathroom to throw up; even the very thought of anyone finding out my psych history fills me with a dread that transports me back into that psych ward with a mat and drain.

In an effort to "get ready", I sit back down at the table and write these eleven words on my statement card:

"I am not afraid to share my story of mental health."

About a year ago that very vision came true! It was the same room, same stage, and same audience as in my vision. I talked about bipolar in front of an audience of hundreds. I did the thing I feared the most.

Now the world's my stage with this book, a book that I never had any intention of writing. That was five years ago this week-end. I am still afraid, but I did it anyway. You might be afraid also, and that's ok. When you are well, and you will be, you might just join me in being crazy enough to think we can change the world.

 End

Aspen's Peer Prescription

What thriving naturally looks like for
a day in the life of a Med Free Bipolar:
(Tear this out of print book!)
Affirmations in AM

10 min on Rebounder/Cellerciser®
While listening to favorite uplifting music
(like "Happy" or "You are a Firework")

1. Himalayan Salt crystals under tongue upon waking with one glass of Water (Or salt brine/sole)
and repeat 10 min before each meal
(or Lemon water or apple cider vinegar or
hydrochloric acid/digestive enzyme supplements)

Eat Breakfast:
(See 100+ great recipes in the
Med Free Bipolar Diet & Cookbook:
coming Spring 2015)
Brain Coffee/Tea
1tbsp grass-fed butter (X-factor)
1tbsp Coconut Oil
1tbsp raw honey (if desired)
Cinnamon/Lavender/Orange essential oil (or not)

Whole/Raw/Almond/Coconut Milk to taste

2. Pop a Happy Pill:
EMPowerplus™ Q96 Multi-vitamin for brain health:
36 vitamins/minerals/aminos and herbs for CALM, COPING, and HAPPINESS
http://www.medfree.myqxlife.com
(Substitute Lithium Orotate/Cell Salts if TRULY can't afford)

3. 500-1000mg Omegas/Essential Fatty Acids & D3
(Fermented Cod Liver Oil with butter oil is best or QOmega, & QD3 spray from QSciences)

4. Probiotic/sleep aid at night: QBiotics or Soil-based like Prescript Assist or Primal Defense

Write down three new things you are grateful for in a gratitude Journal

Read 10 min/day of a good uplifting book
(Like A Fortune to Share by Paul J. Meyer)

That's it! I challenge you to do JUST these things every day for six months!

Overview of the 5 Steps to Med Free Health

Step One: Prepare the Soil

Get plenty of high-quality salt and water every day
Increase HCL and digestive enzymes
Breathe Deeply

Step Two: The Roots of our Health

Eat "dirt" in the form of soil-based probiotics
Eat yoghurt and probiotic-rich foods
Garden, don't sterilize everything
Use Antibiotics only for last-resort emergencies

Step Three: Feed the Crown of the Tree (Brain)

Daily Supplementation
1) Q96 multi-vitamin
(and/or lithium orotate/cell salts)
2) Omega (other fats too like coconut oil)
3) Probiotics (from step 2)
4) Vitamin D3 5-10K IU Spray or liquid form
5) Salt/ Digestive enzymes/HCL with Pepsin
(from Step 1)

6) As needed "stuff" like a sleep aid, Inositol for anxiety, choline for racing thoughts, oils or herbs
(see chapter 12)

Step Four: Clean the Fish Tank:
Detox & Exercise

1) Clean up your outside and inside environment: reduce toxins on skin, detox your insides with herbs, enemas, lithium/mineral salt/ hot springs baths, etc...
2) Exercise on accident by getting active doing something you love. Rebound for 10 min per day!
3) Make small changes in your diet and eat real food

Step Five: Mental Mindset Recovery™:
Overcoming Bipolar PTSD

Habits and behaviors take time to change, so be patient with yourself.
1) Keep a gratitude journal and write down three things before you go to bed each night.
2) Pay attention to your thoughts and self-talk. Increase positivity. Look on the bright side. Read 10 pages of a good personal development book each day.
3) Forgive yourself and others. No one is perfect!
4) Work at something you enjoy (a job or volunteer)
5) Create a Safety Net Plan
6) **Believe** you can recover and **Envision** a better Life!

Each one of these steps is very important. If you don't believe you can be well, all of the other steps might not work. If you skip even a few days of feeding your brain, it will probably act up again. Ask questions on my blog, Facebook, or in a discussion thread on GoodReads. _**Please**_ _leave a review on Amazon._ Thank you and I hope you find joy, peace and healing in your life. *God bless your journey.*

AFTERWORD

Daniel Nuzum, N.D., D.O., D.N., O.M.D

My name is Daniel Nuzum and I am a Board Certified Naturopathic Physician in private practice in Nampa, Idaho. I am married and have four children with my lovely wife, Gina.

My path in natural medicine started as a child. My parents were interested in natural medicine when I was little and I grew up with natural medicine being the primary medicine utilized by my family. I had not been to an M.D. until I needed a physical in high school. My parents and I are all Naturopathic Physicians. I am also a Board Certified Naprapath, a Manual Osteopath, a Mechano-therapist, Doctor of Oriental Medicine, and a Medical Botanist. My parents are Naturopathic Physicians; my dad is also a Mechanotherapist and my mom is a PhD Clinical Nutritionist.

When I was seven years old, my parents embarked on a

fantastic journey that would lead them to adopt 30 plus children. A majority of these children were "crack babies" and came with multiple disabilities, possibly as a result. Their diagnoses ranged from bipolar, autism, cerebral palsy, multiple sclerosis, ADHD, and more. My saintly parents, in their immense love for these suffering children, searched for ways to assist them in their healing process. A majority of these children were "unadoptable" due to their unmanageable behavioral disorders, and in some cases their physical disabilities also. Yes, at times our house was a "mad house," but my parents always waited out the storm and we all survived.

Most of these children were heavily medicated on multiple psychotropic drugs and they still had all the same symptoms. Nothing changed if they took their meds or not. They also suffered extensive side effects. In my experience with 16 of my 32 adopted siblings with bipolar disorder, chemical medicine wasn't effective. One sister had liver failure at fourteen years old due to the three to four anti-psychotic medications, and her bipolar and seizure disorder was still unchanged.

As a result, my parents, after some years of research, devised a program of diet modification, herbal supplements, homeopathic remedies, and nutritional supplementation that had miraculous results with these children with bipolar.

This program is a truly naturopathic approach in that it is entirely holistic, treating the person from as many angles, in as many ways, and on as many levels as possible. Outside of training these children from a Godly-Christian standpoint combined with martial arts training, these are the basics of the program back then, almost identical to the Med Free Method™:

#1- **Diet** - Clean, organic, and macronutrients in the right proportions.

#2- **Digestive health** - Herbal colon and liver cleansing followed by probiotic therapy, not just one time but in a cyclic manner. Remember that 85-95% of the body's serotonin is produced in healthy intestines.

#3- Micronutrients - Enzymatic cofactors necessary for proper brain metabolism. We are the Periodic table walking on two feet.

#4- Homeopathic Remedies

#5- Herbal Nervines (Herbs that support the nervous system, like skullcap)

These are many of the wonderful remedies that Aspen has written about in her book. If you or a loved one suffer from a "chemical imbalance" remember that we are walking Periodic tables and that one or two or five or six chemicals won't balance all the rest. When that whole Periodic table is balanced, you are chemically balanced.

Daniel Nuzum, N.D., D.O., D.N., O.M.D

Recommended & Featured Products

(Prices are approximate at time of printing. Websites and companies subject to change)

The Med Free Method™ is founded on the belief that no one person, doctor, or company has all the answers for every person. I have scoured companies, products, industries, and manufacturing methods to give you the best options I know of, however, I do this as a service to our readers, and take no responsibility for contraindications or adverse reactions.

If someone in a direct sales company gave you this book, please contact them on how best to obtain products.

Supplements:

Chelated Lithium Orotate

Any brands (various qualities) at health food stores or online without a prescription:

http://www.vitaminpartners.com/products/lithium-50-mcg-100-caps

Cell Salts: Local Young Living distributor for AlkiLime or local health food store for Hyland's Bioplasma Cell Salts

For the US, Canada, Australia, Japan and Korea: QSciences has the following recommended products all on one site and carry a money back guarantee:

Contact your local QSciences independent business owner:

http://www.medfree.myqxlife.com

(Please shop here as my wholesale preferred customer only **if** you do not have a distributor or contact the person who gave you this book)

1. EMPowerplus™ Q96 (Foundational Brain Health)

or Qssentials men's or women's pack that includes Q96/ heart/ probiotic/ hormone/ libido herbs

2. QBiotics (For Gut Health)

3. Q Amino Acids (for medication withdrawal)

4. Q Omegas (Essential Fatty Acids for Brain)

5. QSleep, QBoost, QC+

6. QD3 Spray (5,000IU of D3 in 8 sprays)

7. Cellerciser® rebounding equipment

Optional Support if transitioning from medication:
www.micronutrientsupport.com (monthly subscription fee **or** QScience distributors get access free for 1 year for $49.95)

Doctors may also call: 1-888-878-3467

Worldwide: For almost the same brain formula (more expensive and slightly less potent than Q96) but can ship worldwide: See: http://www.hardynutritionals.com/

For racing thoughts:

Q96 Daily

Phosphatidyl Choline: (as needed)

www.truehope.com, online, or most local Health Food Stores

Anxiety

Inositol Powder (do NOT underestimate the power of this one!)

www.truehope.com, online, or most local Health Food Stores

Holy Basil Trinity Blend: Health Food Stores

Fish Oil Supplements:

QOmega (Order above) No burping fish oil!

Fermented Cod Liver Oil, www.greenpasture.org (The capsules are more palatable): Blue Ice Royal with Butter Oil Capsules

Dr. Nuzum's special blends:

(www.nuzumsnaturals.com)

> * Super Earth Energy

> * Inflamagone

> * Digestive Detox

For Sleep:

Lavender Essential Oils

QSleep by QSciences: (see above to order)

GABA Supplements (health food stores)

Vitamin D3

QD3 – D3 is essential for bone health, mental health, vitamin absorption, immune health and works in 2,000 cells in your body. I recommend this spray form: 8 sprays = 5,000 IU or Liquid forms

Reducing Toxins in Home and Garden

www.melaleuca.com (78927935 is my customer #)

Vollara: Water Purifier, Laundry Pure, Air Purifier

www.vollara.com (or your local distributor)

Earth Friendly Alternatives to herbicides, pesticides, and household chemicals

(62-page booklet) www.stonington-gardenclub.org

Recommended Cosmetics and Skin Care /bodywash /shampoo:

Coconut Oil for eye makeup remover and moisturizer

Whole Foods' 365° brand for shampoo/body wash

Ingredient conscious network marketing companies

Superior Food Sources

Bountiful Baskets

www.bountifulbaskets.org

Check your area for availability

Local Farmer's Markets

Recommended Reading

- www.westonprice.org
- www.price-pottenger.org (www.ppnf.org)
- www.gaps.me
- Campbell-McBride, Natasha, M.D., *Gut and Psychology Syndrome*
- Long, Liza, *The Price of Silence: A Mom's Perspective of Metal Illness*
- Ross, Julia, M.A., *The Mood Cure*
- Breggin, Peter R., M.D., and David Cohen, Ph.D., *Your Drug May Be Your Problem*
- Carl Pfeiffer, Ph.D., M.D., *Nutrition and Mental Illness*
- Francis Pottenger, *Pottenger's Cats*
- Rubin, Jordan, *The Maker's Diet* and *Beyond Organic*
- Guyol, Gracelyn, *Healing Depression & Bipolar Disorder Without Drugs*
- Fallon, Sally, *Nourishing Traditions Cookbook* and *Eat Fat, Lose Fat*
- Stringam, Autumn, *A Promise of Hope*
- Dr. Joel D. Wallach & Dr. Ma Lan, *Dead Doctors Don't Lie*
- Weston A. Price, *Nutrition and Physical Degeneration*
- Miklowitz, David J., *The Bipolar Disorder Survival Guide, Second Edition: What You and Your Family Need to Know*
- Fast, Julie, *Bipolar Happens: 35 tips and Tricks to Manage Bipolar Disorder*
- Jamison, Kay Redfield, *An Unquiet Mind*

Acknowledgements

This book took me thirty-two years to write. Twenty years spent living with the disorder that gave me insight, ten years living med free to share how to do it and prove it works, and two years to actually write the book and gain enough courage to talk about it publically. With that being said, there is no way to thank all the people in my life along my path. To all the amazing people in my life, thank you!

To my dad who always brought out the best in me, and my mom who nursed me back to sanity, I love you both so much. Thank you for training me up in the way I should go. To my coaching and publishing team: Maryanna Young, Hannah Cross, Kim Foster, and my fellow authors, thank you for pinning me down when I wanted to run away. Special thanks to Amy Larson for convincing me it is not a good idea to publish anonymously and for all the rest!

To my kids, thank you for your patience, especially Canyon when you said, "Mom, at first I thought this book thing was cool, but I'm pretty much ready for you to be done with it!"

But most importantly, to my husband Chris for supporting my dreams, showing me unconditional love, and inspiring me to be as honorable as he is. I love you and look forward to spending the rest of my life with you!

Look for These Upcoming Books in the Med Free Method™ Book Series

Your Feedback is very important, please leave a review on **Amazon** *and* **Goodreads**

www.facebook.com/medfreebipolar
Twitter: **@medfreebipolar**
www.medfreebipolar.wordpress.com

Endnotes

[1] www.cdc.gov

[2] http://www.americashealthrankings.org/Rankings/InternationalComparisons

[3] http://www.100daysofrealfood.com/2013/02/11/

[4] http://en.wikipedia.org/wiki/Carl_Pfeiffer_(pharmacologist)

[5] Wallach, Joel D., and Ma Lan. 1999. *Dead doctors don't lie*. Franklin, Tenn: Legacy Communications Group.

[6] http://www.mayoclinic.com/health/mental-illness/DS01104/DSECTION=treatments-and-drugs

[7] www.drbroganmd.com

[8] www.cdc.gov

[9] Campbell-McBride, Natasha. 2011. *Gut and psychology syndrome: natural treatment for autism, dyspraxia, A.D.D., dyslexia, A.D.H.D., depression, schizophrenia*. Cambridge, U.K.: Medinform Pub.].

[10] Hart, Leslie. *How the Brain Works*. New York: Basic Books, Publishers, 1975.

[11] Amen, Daniel G. 2000. *Change your brain, change your life: the breakthrough program for conquering anxiety, depression, obsessiveness, anger, and impulsiveness*. New York: Times Books.

[12] http://www.cdc.gov/mentalhealth/basics/burden.htm

[13] Wallach, Joel D., and Ma Lan. 1999. *Dead doctors don't lie*. Franklin, Tenn: Legacy Communications Group.

[14] Ignarro, Louis J. 2005. *No more heart disease: how nitric oxide can prevent--even reverse--heart disease and stroke*. New York: St. Martin's Press.

[15] Berwick, JAMA, 280(15): 1969-1975, 2003

[16] Carl C. Pheiffer, Ph.D., M.D. 1987. *Nutrition and Mental Illness*. Healing Arts Press, Rochester, Vermont.

[17] www.newsecurityaction.org

[18] http://abcnews.go.com/Health/story?id=116701

[19] National Institute on Mental Health (NIMH) at http://www.nimh.nih.gov/

[20] Jamison, Kay R. 1995. *An unquiet mind*. New York: A.A. Knopf. pg. 6.

[21] Hill, Napoleon. 2004. *Think and grow rich*. Los Angeles: Highroads Media

[22] http://www.ncbi.nlm.nih.gov/pmc/articles/PMC3547430/ & http://www.ukapologetics.net/biblicalheart.htm

[23] http://www.marketplace.org/topics/life/big-book/processed-foods-make-70-percent-us-diet

[24] Wright, Jonathan V. 2001. *Why Stomach Acid is Good for You*. M. Evans, Maryland

[25] Campbell-McBride, Natasha. 2011. *Gut and psychology syndrome: natural treatment for autism, dyspraxia, A.D.D., dyslexia, A.D.H.D., depression, schizophrenia*. Cambridge, U.K.: Medinform Pub.

[26] http://news.msn.com/science-technology/fukushima-fallout-should-you-eat-pacific-fish

[27] Wright, Jonathan V. 2001. *Why Stomach Acid is Good for You*. M. Evans, Maryland.

[28] Colbert, Don. 2007. *The Seven pillars of health*. Lake Mary, Fla: Siloam.

[29] De Langre, Jacques. 1994. *Seasalt's Hidden Powers*. Happiness Press.

[30] http://www.globalhealingcenter.com/natural-health/lithium-orotate/

[31] Moore, G.L. Et al Lithium-induced increase in human grey matter, Lancet 2000; 356; 1, 241-242.

[32] Nanaka S, National Academy of Sciences of USA, 1998

[33] Biological Trace Element Research, 1990, by Schrauzer, GN

[34] http://www.catesnutrition.com/improve-your-health-by-eating-more-mindfully/

[35] Bragg, Patricia. 2011. *Super Power Breathing for Super Energy*. Health Science.

[36] http://www.rodalenews.com/running-and-pollution

[37] US Department of Agriculture

[38] http://www.cdc.gov/features/childrensmentalhealth/

[39] Campbell-McBride, Natasha. 2011. *Gut and psychology syndrome: natural treatment for autism, dyspraxia, A.D.D., dyslexia, A.D.H.D., depression, schizophrenia*. Cambridge, U.K.: Medinform Pub.

[40] Rubin, Jordan. 2004. *The Maker's diet*. Lake Mary, Fla: Siloam.

[41] Campbell-McBride, Natasha. 2011. *Gut and psychology syndrome: natural treatment for autism, dyspraxia, A.D.D., dyslexia, A.D.H.D., depression, schizophrenia*. Cambridge, U.K.: Medinform Pub.].

[42] http://www.judytsafrirmd.com/an-effective-probiotic-prescript-assist/

[43] Gershon, Michael D. 1999. *The second brain*. New York: HarperCollins World

[44] www.chriskesser.com

[45] Campbell-McBride, Natasha. 2011. *Gut and psychology syndrome: natural treatment for autism, dyspraxia, A.D.D., dyslexia, A.D.H.D., depression, schizophrenia*. Cambridge, U.K.: Medinform Pub.].

[46] JAMA, 2002; 287:3127-9; What Doctors Don't Tell You Magazine, December 2002

[47] Kaplan et al, 2001, p. 942

[48] Pheiffer, C. Carl, Ph.D., M.D. 1987. *Nutrition and Mental Illness*. Healing Arts Press, Rochester, Vermont, 1987, pg. 67

[49] Campbell-McBride, Natasha. 2011. *Gut and psychology syndrome: natural treatment for autism, dyspraxia, A.D.D., dyslexia, A.D.H.D., depression, schizophrenia*. Cambridge, U.K.: Medinform Pub.].

[50] Amen, Daniel G. 2000. *Change your brain, change your life: the breakthrough program for conquering anxiety, depression, obsessiveness, anger, and impulsiveness*. New York: Times Books.

[51] Wallach, Joel D., and Ma Lan. 1999. *Dead doctors don't lie*. Franklin, Tenn: Legacy Communications Group.

[52] Lake, James, and David Spiegel. 2007. *Complementary and alternative treatments in mental health care*. Washington, DC: American Psychiatric Pub.

[53] Lake, James, and David Spiegel. 2007. *Complementary and alternative treatments in mental health care*. Washington, DC: American Psychiatric Pub.

[54] Fallon, Sally, Mary G. Enig, Kim Murray, and Marion Dearth. 2001. *Nourishing traditions: the cookbook that challenges politically correct nutrition and the diet dictocrats*. Washington, DC: NewTrends Pub.

[55] Morgan Abramson, "NutriGenomics of Gingko Bilboa", www.alpha-genetics.com

[56] Lake, James, and David Spiegel. 2007. *Complementary and alternative treatments in mental health care*. Washington, DC: American Psychiatric Pub.

[57] Campbell-McBride, Natasha. 2011. *Gut and psychology syndrome: natural treatment for autism, dyspraxia, A.D.D., dyslexia, A.D.H.D., depression, schizophrenia*. Cambridge, U.K.: Medinform Pub.].

[58] Dr. Brogan's Online Course - Beyond Medication: Mental Health, Holistic Healing & Nutrition: http://www.greenmedinfo.com/event/beyond-medication-mental-health-holistic-healing?a=69165

[59] Campbell-McBride, Natasha. 2011. *Gut and psychology syndrome: natural treatment for autism, dyspraxia, A.D.D., dyslexia, A.D.H.D., depression, schizophrenia*. Cambridge, U.K.: Medinform Pub.

[60] Rubin, Jordan. 2004. *The Maker's diet*. Lake Mary, Fla: Siloam

[61] http://blogs.nicholas.duke.edu/thegreengrok/insearchoftsca5

[62] Campbell-McBride, Natasha. 2011. *Gut and psychology syndrome: natural treatment for autism, dyspraxia, A.D.D., dyslexia, A.D.H.D., depression, schizophrenia*. Cambridge, U.K.: Medinform Pub.].

[63] http://www.doctoroz.com/videos/your-sunscreen-might-be-poisoning-you

[64] Colbert, Don. 2007. *The Seven pillars of health*. Lake Mary, Fla: Siloam. pg. 117

[65] NASA report published in the *Journal of Applied Physiology* 49(5): 881-887, 1980

[66] http://rebound-air.com/best_rebounding_33_ways.htm

[67] Wallach, Joel D., and Ma Lan. 1999. *Dead doctors don't lie*. Franklin, Tenn: Legacy Communications Group.

[68] http://www.psychologytoday.com/blog/the-human-beast/201103/faith-healing-shouldnt-work-it-does

[69] http://psychologytoday.com/blog/science-isnt-golden/201109/full-disclosure-needed-about-psychiatric-drugs-shorten-life

[70] Pfeiffer, Carl Curt. 1987. *Nutrition and mental illness: an orthomolecular approach to balancing body chemistry*. Rochester, Vt: Healing Arts Press.

[71] http://fountainheadclinic.com/circadian.htm

[72] Lake, James, and David Spiegel. 2007. *Complementary and alternative treatments in mental health care*. Washington, DC: American Psychiatric Pub. Pg. 365

[73] Lake, James, and David Spiegel. 2007. *Complementary and alternative treatments in mental health care*. Washington, DC: American Psychiatric Pub. Pg. 365

[74] http://www.nbcnews.com/id/8318894/ns/health-health_care/t/survey-most-doctors-believe-god-afterlife/#.UgFGp2TtgVk

[75] Lake, James, and David Spiegel. 2007. *Complementary and alternative treatments in mental health care*. Washington, DC: American Psychiatric Pub. Pg. 366.

[76] Lake, James, and David Spiegel. 2007. *Complementary and alternative treatments in mental health care*. Washington, DC: American Psychiatric Pub. Pg. 366.
[77] Dotter, Americus. 2012. *Soul Sale: A Rude Awakening*. Kindle Edition. pp. 241-242.

[78] http://www.reiki.org/reikipractice/practicehomepage.html

[79] Gopi Krishna. 1975. *The awakening of Kundalini*. New York: Dutton. Pg. 124

[80]http://www.nutritionalhealing.com.au/content/articlescontent.php?heading=Acetylchol ine%20deficiency

[81] Sahelian, Ray. 1996. *DHEA: a practical guide*. Garden City Park, N.Y.: Avery Pub. Group. Pg. 16

[82] Sahelian, Ray. 1996. *DHEA: a practical guide*. Garden City Park, N.Y.: Avery Pub. Group. Pg. 1

[83] http://www.webmd.com/depression/guide/serotonin-syndrome-causes-symptoms-treatments

[84] Sahelian, Ray. 1996. *DHEA: a practical guide*. Garden City Park, N.Y.: Avery Pub. Group

[85] Morales and Yen study. 1994, University of California, San Diego, School of Medicine

Additional Resources

Trudeau, Kevin. 2004. *Natural cures "they" don't want you to know about*. Elk Grove Village, IL: Alliance Pub. Group.

Ryan, M. J. 1999. *Attitudes of gratitude*. New York, N.Y.: MJF Books.

Pottenger, Francis Marion, and Weston A. Price. 2007. *Story of the Price-Pottenger Nutrition Foundation*. Phoenix, AZ: Morley Video Productions.

Pottenger, Francis M., Elaine Pottenger, and Robert T. Pottenger. 1983. *Pottenger's cats: a study in nutrition*. La Mesa, CA (P.O. Box 2614, La Mesa 92041): Price-Pottenger Nutrition Foundation.

Graham, Gray, Deborah Kesten, and Larry Scherwitz. 2011. *Pottenger's prophecy: how food resets genes for wellness or illness*. Amherst, Mass: White River Press.

Moore GJ, JM Bebchuk, IB Wilds, G Chen, and HK Manji. 2000. "Lithium-induced increase in human brain grey matter". *Lancet*. 356 (9237): 1241-2.

Schrauzer GN, and KP Shrestha. 1990. "Lithium in drinking water and the incidences of crimes, suicides, and arrests related to drug addictions". *Biological Trace Element Research*. 25 (2): 105-13.

Simkin, Debra R., and Charles W. Popper. 2012. *Alternative and Complementary Therapies for Children with Psychiatric Disorders, An Issue of Child and Adolescent Psychiatric Clinics of North America*. London: Elsevier Health Sciences. http://public.eblib.com/EBLPublic/PublicView.do?ptiID=1431090.

Stoll, Andrew L. 2001. *The omega-3 connection: the groundbreaking omega-3 antidepression diet and brain program*. New York: Simon & Schuster.

Hoffer, Abram. 1999. *Orthomolecular treatment for schizophrenia: megavitamin supplements and nutritional strategies for healing and recovery*. Los Angeles: Keats Pub.

Edelman, Eva. 2001. *Natural healing for schizophrenia: and other common mental disorders*. Eugene, Or: Borage Books.

Nagel, Ramiel. 2009. *Cure tooth decay: heal & prevent cavities with nutrition*. Los Gatos, CA: Golden Child Pub.

Meletis, Chris D., and Jason E. Barker. 2004. *Herbs and nutrients for the mind: a guide to natural brain enhancers*. Westport, Conn: Praeger.

Marohn, Stephanie. 2003. *The natural medicine guide to bipolar disorder*. Charlottesville, Va: Hampton Roads Pub. Co.